ENCOUNTER ON THE MOON

BY
ROBIN MOORE

KING*fisher*

KINGFISHER
An imprint of Kingfisher Publications Plc
New Penderel House
283-288 High Holborn
London WC1V7HZ

First published by Kingfisher Publications Plc 1996

10 9 8 7 6 5 4 3

A CIP catalogue record for this book is available from the British Library

ISBN 0 7534 0025 1

"You will have to make your own minds up about how much of the 'facts'
contained in this story are true. Some are based on public information, but
others are the result of a fictional interpretation by the author of events, what
might have been said or done. Some names have been changed, as you can see,
to protect the individuals involved."

Designed and typeset by the Harrington Consultancy Ltd, Unit 14, 37–42
Compton Street, London EC1V 0AP
Printed in the United Kingdom

CONTENTS PAGE

INTRODUCTION

The world abounds with physical phenomena that can be analyzed, measured, even visited by tourists. Phenomena such as the pyramids that exist in various parts of the world or the complex geometric markings in the Alti Plano in South America. But even though these spectacles are *real,* we can only guess as to their true purpose. So imagine how much more difficult it is to prove an *inexplicable* experience or the fleeting glimpse of an unidentifiable object? The answer is, of course, that it is virtually impossible.

For almost half a century, stories of alien encounters and strange sightings have become part of our "reality." Most can be explained away as wild imaginings or, at best, optical illusions. But there are some accounts that have seemingly defied explanation, or have simply never been explained at all.

One such story took place quietly, behind the scenes of a spectacular 20 th century adventure. For, as the world watched the Apollo 11 Moon landing and Neil Armstrong's "one small step for man," there was quite possibly another adventure unfolding that the public were not privy to.

Were the Apollo 11 astronauts being watched by alien spacecraft during their ground-breaking mission? Did they inform Houston of their dilemma, and what exactly did ground control decide to do? Where is the evidence that would confirm that the first Moon landing was far more astounding than NASA had ever planned it to be?

That evidence has never published. Instead, the truth has been hidden away in dusty files or in computer databases. Governments prohibit access to these most secret of files. Files marked:

CHAPTER ONE

My name is Harrison Grear.

Maybe you've heard of me. You might have seen some of my "Space Watch" columns in the *Houston Sentinel*. If you haven't, you can just say so. It won't hurt my feelings. Believe me, after 30 years in the newspaper business, I've become as thick-skinned as an old bull elephant.

My distinguished colleagues down at the newsroom say I have the temperament of one, too. I know what they think of me. They tease me sometimes by calling me "Hard News Harry." They think I'm old-fashioned.

I guess they're right. I *am* old-fashioned. When I got into this business, a reporter was a person with a sharp pencil, a spiral-bound notebook, and a memory like a—well, like an elephant.

Most of these modern-day journalists couldn't cover a Sunday school picnic without $10,000 worth of electronic equipment. They wouldn't know a real news story if they fell over one in the street.

When I was writing the front page, I took pride in my stories. Nowadays, most of what the *Sentinel* publishes isn't news at all: It's just scandal and gossip, a never-ending clothesline of dirty laundry hung out for all to see.

It wasn't always this way. Back in my day, the city editor was Ben Haley, a cigar-chomping tyrant who wanted the facts—hard, fast, and accurate—and no funny business.

He was loud and abrasive, not exactly the nurturing type. But, by God, he taught me to write! He taught me to write about the things that mattered—stories about struggle in adversity and overcoming impossible odds; stories that brought people together; stories that celebrated all the joy and pain of human life. Nowadays, all we do is argue about sports scores and peek into the bedrooms of the stars.

I don't mean to sound bitter—in many ways I've been very lucky. The newspaper business has been good to me. For three decades, I've covered the space industry, which is big news in this town. Because the Manned Spacecraft Center is right here in Houston, I've had a front-row seat for some of the most exciting chapters in the history of space exploration.

To anyone who wasn't alive during the glory years of the Space

Race, it's impossible to convey the excitement everyone felt with each liftoff and launch. Sometimes, it almost felt as if we were all strapped into the cockpit together, feeling the burn of the engines beneath us, our helmeted faces turned toward the distant stars.

Every mission carried our young astronauts farther into the new frontiers of space. I wrote story after story, each one more amazing than the last.

But there is one story I've never released to the public—until now.

It happened back in 1969, the year our men walked on the Moon.

As far as I know, I am the only journalist who had any inkling of what was really going on. You see, while the other reporters were depending on canned press releases fed to them by the NASA public affairs officer, I had a source on the inside. My Uncle Pete, my father's brother, worked as a technician in Building 30 at Mission Control—and he gave me the real scoop, just as it happened.

When I heard the story, my first impulse was to rush to the typewriter and hammer out the incredible details, then dash straight down to Ben's office and blurt the whole thing out.

But something held me back. I knew deep down that Ben would never let me run the story. It was full of holes. I didn't have a single documentable fact. All I had was a handful of tantalizing leads and the testimony of an "unnamed source." There was no way I could quote Uncle Pete—it would have cost him his job.

So I killed the story, killed it dead. I never showed it to Ben. The truth is, I just chickened out.

But now that I'm about to retire, I've acquired a new courage. Old Ben and Uncle Pete are in their graves now, and I have become an old man myself—an old man with a story to tell.

So now, with retirement staring me in the face, I think I am finally ready to publish this forbidden story—*whatever* the consequences.

In the meantime, I've revived my boyish interest in science fiction.

It started back in the 1950s when I was a kid in Amarillo, Texas. Every night I'd spend hours reading under the bedcovers by flashlight—devouring dog-eared paperback novels with titles like *They Came from Mars* and *War on Distant Planets*.

It was through those far-fetched stories that my young mind began, for the first time, to grapple with the exciting question of what was really waiting for us out there in the vastness of deep space.

I guess that wide-eyed boy is still alive in me, somewhere. Many nights, after my wife has gone to bed, I sit up late in my favorite chair down in the den, reading books by science fiction authors such as Asimov, Sagan, and Clarke. On those evenings, when the house is dark and quiet—with just the rattling of the heat pipes and the ticking of the clock on the mantlepiece to keep me company—my imagination takes flight and I am a boy again, dreaming about exploring the silent darkness of space. For a while, I float weightlessly through the universe, held in the magic of that dream.

Reading these books makes me feel humble, it really does. Because I now understand that the sci-fi writers have, in many ways, done a far better job of explaining the mysteries of the universe than we journalists.

They say that every newspaper reporter has a half-finished novel tucked away in his desk drawer somewhere. Maybe that's true, or at least it is for me. Anyway, because I can't prove that what I am about to tell you is absolutely true, I'm not going to present it as journalism. Instead, I've decided just to tell my story and let you decide for yourself how much is fact and how much is fiction.

So here it is—an attempt to strike some kind of blow at the truth.

If this story is simply fiction, then no harm is done. It'll be just like one more piece of space junk, circling the planet.

But if this story is fact—then what?

CHAPTER TWO

July 11, 1969

Apollo 11 Commander Neil Armstrong gripped the controls of the Lunar Module, his gaze fixed on the numbers dancing across the instrument panel. At his side, keeping a close watch on the altimeter, was his crewmate, Buzz Aldrin. According to the readout, they were only 4,500 feet above the surface of the Moon.

Armstrong flicked an overhead switch. An insistent beeping filled the landing craft.

"What are you doing?" Aldrin asked sharply.

"I don't like the way we're coming in," Armstrong replied. "I'm going to override the navigational computer and land the Lunar Module manually."

"Are you sure?" asked Aldrin. He could see that they were losing altitude at a dangerous rate.

"No problem." Armstrong's voice was confident.

'Well,' Aldrin thought to himself, 'he *is* probably NASA's best pilot. I guess he knows what he's doing.' But the thought did little to comfort him. According to the flickering readout in front of them, they were dropping at the alarming rate of 100 feet per second.

"All right," Armstrong muttered, "let's bring her in steady."

At that moment, a tense voice from Mission Control crackled over the radio lines:

"ABORT! ABORT! You're coming in too fast!"

"I'm okay," Armstrong growled into his mouthpiece, "I've got it."

The urgent voice crackled back from Houston: "NEGATIVE! BE ADVISED—YOU ARE ABOUT TO CRASH! FIRE YOUR ASCENT ROCKET! HIT THE ABORT HANDLE NOW!"

"Our altitude is only 100 feet," Aldrin said urgently, "50 feet lower and we're in the 'dead man's zone'. After that, we can't abort, Neil. Neil...NEIL?"

"I've got it," Armstrong muttered through clenched teeth.

But he *didn't* have it. Mission Control was right; they were coming in way too fast.

A second later, the altimeter ran into negative numbers and the flickering screen went dead.

They had crashed on the surface of the Moon.

"Well, Neil," Aldrin said acidly, "thanks to you, we're dead. And the LM is a pile of scrap metal."

"Relax," Armstrong said calmly, "I'll get it right next time."

The lights in the simulator control room went on, and one of the NASA technicians opened the door. "You guys wanna try it again?" he asked.

"In a few minutes," Armstrong said, "just let me reset these switches."

The technician closed the door.

"Tell me this," Buzz said hotly, "why didn't you abort when they told you to?"

Armstrong was flicking a series of overhead switches.

"Because I wanted to see if I could pull it off—without aborting. I just had a gut feeling that I could do it."

"Well, you were wrong. Your 'gut feeling' got us killed. We don't have time to fool about like this. Neil, how are you going to land this thing on the Moon next week?"

Armstrong turned quickly to face his partner.

"I'm going to practice," he said coolly.

Aldrin fought back rising anger. With only five days left before the launch, Armstrong still hadn't been able to land the LM simulator safely. And this wasn't the only problem. It was just one of thousands of potentially disastrous trouble spots, only one of thousands of things that could go wrong.

Ever since March, the Apollo crew had been hard at work in the Command Module and Lunar Module simulators at Cape Kennedy, Florida. Working with a dedicated staff of technicians and scientists, they had been putting in ten, sometimes 14-hour days, slogging through the grueling task of preparing themselves and their spacecraft for the journey to the Moon.

On Fridays, the pilots would hop into their T-38s and drive back to their families in Houston, Texas, for a hurried weekend at home. Then, first thing on Monday morning, it was straight back to the Cape.

Now the stress was beginning to show. Tempers were wearing

thin and time was running out. People were scared. Even though Mission Commander Armstrong had told the press just last week that they were ready to go to the Moon, privately everyone had their doubts.

"Hey fellas!" It was the voice of Mike Collins, the third member of the crew, coming in over the intercom. "Guess who's here? Jim Lovell."

Lovell was one of the most respected astronauts on the Cape. He and Frank Borman had flown the Gemini 7 mission, which had orbited the Earth for a record-breaking 14 days. He had flown with Aldrin on Gemini 12 in 1966 when Buzz had made his highly successful space walks. He had also served as senior pilot for the three-man Apollo 8 mission the year before. What's more, Lovell was commander of the backup crew for Apollo 11.

When Aldrin opened the door, Lovell was standing there with his hands in his pockets, grinning from ear to ear.

"How's it going?" he asked cheerfully.

Aldrin rolled his eyes.

Lovell frowned.

"That bad, huh? Well, if it's any consolation, Apollo 8 was the same way. I didn't think we were ever going to be ready."

Armstrong stepped from the simulator and shook hands with Lovell.

"Did you make a special trip out here to see us?" he asked.

The astronaut nodded. "Yeah. Deke Slayton invited me to have lunch with you guys today. He's waiting for us down in the staff room."

Mike Collins joined them as they filed down the hallway toward the dining facility.

Chief Astronaut Deke Slayton was the mother hen for the Apollo 11 crew. Whenever things looked bleak, he could always be counted on to do something to boost morale. He understood how these men felt.

Slayton was a legend in the Space Program. He was an old-fashioned, hell-for-leather test pilot, one of the original seven Mercury astronauts. By rights, he should have been to the Moon and back by now. But he had been grounded by the medics for an irregular heartbeat and had never got any closer to the heavens than his console at Mission Control. Because NASA realized that the pilots would relate better to one of their own kind, they put Slayton in charge of all the flight crews.

Deke watched the astronauts come into the small dining room with their meal trays. He closed the door behind them. He and Lovell sat at on one side of a long table, the Apollo crew on the other.

Slayton glanced across the table at his crew as they dug into their green beans and potatoes. It occurred to him that they looked almost like brothers, as if they had been cast from the same mold: close-cropped hair; rugged faces; big, capable hands. They were even wearing identical NASA jumpsuits.

But he knew that inside, each man was different. That was why he had teamed them with each other—so that the strengths of one made up for the weaknesses of another.

Although sometimes headstrong, Neil had the vital nerve and intuition needed to pilot the Lunar Module. He would be able to stay calm under the intense pressure of the Apollo mission and also had the skill to pilot the craft manually if anything went wrong. Perhaps it was his vast experience that gave Buzz the maturity of character to handle Armstrong. But Aldrin also had the extensive knowledge and sound reasoning that could make the difference between life and death. Deke glanced at Mike Collins who was eagerly gulping down his meal. Mike was the most easy-going of the three men. Even so, his role was no less crucial. While Armstrong and Aldrin explored the lunar surface, Collins would be orbiting the Moon in the Command Module waiting to link up with them before the journey back to Earth. It was up to Collins to be there at the right time or the other two crew members would be stuck out there forever. Deke shuddered at the thought. Yet despite the dangers of the mission, he felt confident that he had picked the only crew for the job.

"You fellas look like you haven't eaten for weeks!" Slayton said with a crooked grin.

It wasn't really funny, but everyone laughed anyway. It helped to dispel some of the tension they were feeling.

Slayton's face became serious again. He paused for a while before speaking. "Listen guys, it's time we faced facts: There is no way you are going to be able to land that piece of tinfoil and chicken wire on the Moon in only five days' time. I recommend that we postpone the launch for at least a month."

Forks and spoons stopped in midair. Test pilots never like to show they are surprised by anything, but for a moment all three men looked as if Slayton had hit them in the face with a bucket of of cold water.

"It's nothing to be ashamed of," Lovell said soothingly. "Sure, the press will howl about it. But nobody in NASA will think the worse of you guys if you hold off for a while."

"I don't care what the press or anybody says," Slayton put in, "I'm not sending you guys up there until you're sure you're ready."

There was a long silence. Each man turned his thoughts over slowly.

Buzz Aldrin broke a roll in half and began smearing butter on it.

"I have a lot of concerns," he admitted, "but I don't think it makes sense to delay the launch."

He glanced at his crewmates, sitting on either side of him.

"I don't know about you guys, but I've spent over 400 hours in that simulator and I think if I have to go in there one more time, I'm going to throw up. I am just about out of patience with this preflight stuff. If we keep going at this pace, we're going to be too exhausted to handle the mission. I think we need to sort out our problems and get on with the launch."

Mike Collins nodded. "I think Buzz is right. We need to push on through this slump we're in and get operational. I don't think that it's impossible. But I do think we need to pull ourselves together— and fast. I don't know if this will help," he said, reaching into his top pocket, "but I've been working on a list here of what I consider to be the most critical problems we face on this voyage. Would you like to hear what I've written?"

Slayton nodded. "Go ahead, Mike."

Collins unfolded his notes and smoothed the paper out on the table top.

"Number One: The Launch. Obviously a lot can go wrong here, but it's basically out of our hands. It'll be a very tense 11 minutes from the time we leave the launch pad until we are in orbit around the Earth.

"Number Two: The Trans-Lunar Injection. The Saturn rocket will reignite and blast us out of Earth's orbit and set us on the proper trajectory for our three-day journey to the Moon. If we don't do this right, the chances are we won't get back to Earth at all.

"Number Three: Lunar Orbit Insertion. We will have to make two pretty precise burns here: One to slow us down enough to be captured by the Moon's gravity; another to keep us far enough from the Moon to avoid crashing into it.

"Number Four: Descent Orbit Insertion. Here Buzz and Neil will climb into the Lunar Module and make their descent from the Command Module, leaving me to orbit the Moon while they head down to the surface. If we don't get it right, the LM could land in the wrong place. Or it could miss the Moon *entirely.* I don't even want to to think about what we would do about that."

Slayton took a sip of coffee. "Remind me to talk with you guys about that later. Go on, Mike."

"Number Five: The Lunar Landing. Could be very dangerous. We don't really know what the surface is like. The LM could be buried in a bottomless pit of ash or could crash into bedrock. Also, magnetic potholes could play havoc with the navigational computer—if that happens, you guys will have to fly without instruments.

"Number Six: Walking on the Moon. This is the biggest unknown. There might be pressure cracks or underground lava tubes that would cause the surface to collapse beneath you. Besides that, we know the surface of the Moon is constantly being bombarded with cosmic rays and small meteorites. It's possible that these could tear holes in your protective suits, or even in the fabric walls of the LM. Exposure to the lunar environment would mean instant death."

Aldrin was thoughtfully buttering a second roll. As Mike was talking, he could feel the odds mounting up against them.

"Number Seven: LM Liftoff. There is only one engine and it had better work. Otherwise, you guys will be stranded there on the lunar surface until your oxygen runs out. I'll be orbiting 60 miles above you—there won't be anything I can do to bring you back."

Here Collins paused briefly and took a sip of lukewarm coffee. He looked over at Armstrong, who was calmly carving at his roast beef with a steak knife. Collins never could figure out what that guy was thinking.

"Number Eight: LM Rendezvous with the CM. I'll need to be in precisely the right place to capture and dock with you guys in orbit.

"Number Nine: Trans-Earth Injection. Once we're all in the CM again, we jettison the LM and do a one-engine burn to get us back home.

"Number Ten: Reentry. We'll have to enter the Earth's atmosphere at exactly the right angle for a successful splashdown. Also, the parachute had better open, and the frogmen have to be ready to retrieve us and get us safely back to the aircraft carrier."

There were a few moments of silence after Collins finished reading out his list. He had given everyone a lot to think about.

Then Buzz spoke up. "Well, Mike, we can always count on you to cheer us up when the going gets tough!"

Everyone allowed themselves a grin.

"There is one other thing," Collins said seriously, folding the paper and stuffing it into his pocket, "I think the biggest hazards are the ones we haven't even prepared for, the ones that are totally unknown and unanticipated."

"I guess we'll just have to face those when we come to them," Buzz muttered.

Slayton laced his fingers across his knee and leaned back in his chair. "So what do you say fellows? It's your decision. I told you what I think, but I'm going to leave it up to you."

There was one man who hadn't spoken yet.

"I agree with Buzz and Mike," Armstrong said. "But for a different reason. The way I see it, we're in a race with the Soviets —pure and simple. We don't know how close they are to putting a man up there. I wish we did, but we don't. If we delay another month, it could cost us the Moon. The last thing I want to do is get up there and find a Soviet flag planted on the lunar surface. I say we go ahead as planned."

"We all feel the same way, Neil, but safety is the top priority," said Slayton. "But if you all think you're ready..."

Neil interrupted him. "We want to go *now* Deke."

"Is that unanimous?" Slayton asked.

"I'm GO," said Aldrin.

"I think we can do it," said Collins.

"GO," said Armstrong.

"Then I think you should know that there are a few other

concerns—things that you should know about before we send you guys up there," Slayton said.

"What do you mean, Deke?" Armstrong asked.

Slayton took a deep breath, then plunged ahead.

"I suppose you've all heard rumors about strange—how can I say this?—strange 'happenings' on some of the previous flights."

"What kind of 'happenings'?" Aldrin asked.

Slayton shot a quick glance at Lovell.

"Go ahead, Deke," Lovell said, "they have a right to know."

"Fellas, I will come straight to the point. You need to be aware of the UFO factor."

There was a moment of stunned silence. Then all three astronauts burst into hysterical laughter.

Slayton and Lovell sat upright and serious in their chairs.

The astronauts hadn't laughed so much in weeks. They knew that every now and then, when things got tense and crews were overworked, it was an old NASA tradition for someone to play some outrageous practical joke.

"Well, guys," Armstrong said, as he wiped the tears of laughter from his eyes, "I guess if we meet anyone up there, we'll just have to invite them into the LM for a cup of coffee and a piece of pie."

That sent Aldrin and Collins into a fresh wave of uproarious laughter.

At last, Slayton brought his fist down hard on the top of the table.

"Knock it off!" he said sharply.

As suddenly as it had begun, the laughter stopped. In the ringing silence that followed, it slowly dawned on the crew of Apollo 11 that this time Slayton and Lovell were not joking.

CHAPTER THREE

"Deke," Armstrong said, "you can't be serious about this."

But Slayton nodded solemnly.

"I'm deadly serious," he said. "Several of our spacecraft have been followed by unidentified flying objects. Every time this has occurred, the pilots have informed Mission Control. Obviously, the public has been kept in the dark as far as is possible. The last thing NASA wants is a panic among the general public.

"Besides," Slayton added with a sly grin, "I don't think the people at the top like the idea that there are things flying around out there that we can't explain. They don't have the answers, so they don't want any questions."

Slayton studied the faces of the crew. They stared back, unconvinced.

"Look," he went on, "I know what you're thinking. I know you think this whole thing is a pile of garbage. I know how you feel about this stuff. I suppose every pilot has seen something in his career that he could call a UFO. Heck, I saw one myself back in 1951, when I was testing a P-51 fighter jet over Minneapolis.

"I was flying at about 10,000 feet on a bright, sunny afternoon, when I saw an object up ahead that I thought, at first, was a kid's kite. Then I realized that no kite could fly that high. As I got closer, it started to look more like a disk. But this thing wasn't just hanging there in the sky; it was moving away from me. There I was, flying at about 300 miles an hour, and this thing was zipping away from me like I was standing still. I tracked it for a while. Then, all of a sudden, the darned thing just took off. It pulled a 45 degree climbing turn, accelerated, and just flat disappeared.

"I guess I did what just about every pilot does when he sees something like that—I tried to convince myself that it didn't really happen. But men, I have been in the Space Program too long and seen too much to discount the possibility of UFOs. And besides, I have personally interviewed the astronauts who have made the sightings. I am not saying that we know what they saw. But I'll tell you this, boys: You can't just brush this thing aside. *Something* is going on up there."

Aldrin shook his head, "I'm not buying this," he said, "I'd like to talk to one of these pilots who says he's sighted a UFO."

Slayton nodded. "I figured you would," he said, "that's why I invited Jim over today."

Collins shook his head in disbelief.

"Come on, Jim," he said, "don't tell us you're in on this, too?"

Lovell spread his hands and leaned back in his chair.

"I know," he said soothingly, "I know this whole thing sounds nuts. But it's for real, guys. We just thought you should know the whole story before we sent you up there."

"Let me get this straight," Aldrin said, "are you telling me that you were tailed by a UFO?"

Lovell nodded.

"On Gemini 7, back in '65, we were in orbit for 14 days so we had plenty of time to make observations. We were definitely being followed. Shortly after we left the Earth's atmosphere, we saw a shiny object on our tail.

"I reported it to Mission Control. They told me that what I was seeing was our own jettisoned booster rocket, falling away from us. But I told them, loud and clear, that this was something else. We never figured out what it was. But it sure stayed with us for a long time.

"I also spotted a similar craft on the Apollo 8 mission last year. By then I was convinced that something strange was going on. But we were strictly forbidden to discuss it with you guys until you absolutely needed to know. Well, you need to know now."

Armstrong sat back in his chair, a smile playing at the corners of his lips.

"All right, all right," he said gamely, "suppose we go along with this for a minute, just for the sake of discussion. Let's say that these UFOs are spaceships of extraterrestrial origin. Let's say they're being flown by pilots from another planet. Let's say they cross flight paths with us. What the heck are we supposed to do about it?"

"First of all," Slayton answered, "you should know that none of the UFOs have displayed any aggression toward us. They just seem to be watching, keeping an eye on us. So we don't think you'll be in any danger during the flight.

"The main thing is, if you see anything unusual, anything at all, we want you to report it to Mission Control. Like I said, we don't want to frighten any members of the public, so you'll have to use a system of code words. Remember, millions of people will be watching you on their TV sets. Newsmen will be scrutinizing your every word."

"The code words we've worked out to indicate the presence of alien spacecraft are 'Santa Claus'. I think Wally Schirra on Mercury 8 was the first to use them. Jim used them as well, on Apollo 8."

Lovell grinned as he remembered. "It was Christmas day when we came out from behind the dark side of the Moon," he said. "I said to Houston: 'Please be informed: There is a Santa Claus.' I guess the public took it as some kind of holiday greeting. But people in Mission Control knew that it meant something entirely different."

Slayton nodded.

"You guys can do the same. If you see anything strange, just say 'Santa Claus' and we'll take you off the general transmission channel right away. That way, the whole world won't be eavesdropping on our conversation."

"Do you think the public is going to be that interested?" Collins asked.

"They sure will—and we have to keep them interested," Slayton answered. "If we want the funding for the Space Program to continue, we have to convince the public that their money is well spent. They've paid $13 billion to see you guys walk on the Moon. We have to give them what they've paid for."

"It's funny," Lovell said, "I remember back in '61, when President Kennedy started this whole thing off by giving NASA the task of putting a man on the Moon by the end of the decade. We didn't think it was possible. Heck, in those days, our rockets were exploding on the launch pad!

"But we've come so far, guys. It's within our reach. And you fellas are going to be carrying the flag for us. With only 169 days to go until Kennedy's deadline, you guys are going to be the ones to make it happen."

Slayton smiled.

"The news organizations have predicted that about one-fifth of the global population will be glued to their TV sets, watching everything you do, listening to every word you say. So, if you do see anything strange, keep cool, calm, and collected.

As soon as we get you off-line, we'll evaluate the situation and advise you as best we can. Remember that I'll be there at Mission Control, just a phone call away. I'll stick with you, whatever happens. Any questions?"

Looking a little overwhelmed, the Apollo crew shook their heads.

"All right, fellas," Slayton said,. "let's get back to the simulator. We've still got a lot of work to do. We're going to the Moon!"

CHAPTER FOUR

It had been a long day for the crew of Apollo 11. That night, they retired to their quarters on Merritt Island, in the NASA complex on the Cape. This was a small apartment with a kitchen, a living room, and a few bedrooms. Despite the day's unexpected turn of events, none of the astronauts felt much like talking. They simply mumbled their good nights and headed to their separate rooms, eager to capture a few hours of much-needed sleep.

But sleep did not come easily, especially for Buzz Aldrin. He was an intelligent and introspective man—some people said *too* introspective for his own good. He was not an easy man to get to know. He always seemed to be locked in some kind of intense conflict, both with himself and with those around him.

Aldrin's path to the Space Program had been a unique one: He was born Edwin Eugene Aldrin in Montclair, New Jersey. As a child, his penchant for thinking and talking had earned him the nickname "Buzz." The name was to follow him into adult life. He was a veteran of the Korean War and had flown 66 combat missions for the air force.

He was unique among astronauts because he had earned a doctorate in aeronautics from MIT University and had written his thesis on Manned Orbital Rendezvous. He put his theories into practice in 1966 when he and Lovell had piloted Gemini 12. Aldrin left the craft three times on that mission, walking in space for a total of five and a half hours, and assisted in the successful docking of two spacecraft.

Sometimes, when Aldrin had trouble sleeping, he would remember how it had felt to float about in the zero-gravity of blue space, attached to the ship only by a tether cord. For some reason he couldn't explain, this memory always brought him a deep sense of peace and contentment, a feeling almost like being an infant, drifting around in the fluid of the womb.

The Apollo Mission had certainly given him plenty of sleepless nights. The general exhaustion of their grueling training schedule had taken its toll. Added to that there were the usual prelaunch jitters.

And then there was the thing that had recently caused him the most anguish—the misunderstanding between him and Armstrong about who was going to be the first man to walk on the Moon.

It was obvious that the first man to set foot on the lunar surface would be assured a place in the history books. The second man would quickly be forgotten. While it was true that the Apollo crew members were a team, they were also test pilots and, true to their type, they were intensely competitive. Aldrin wanted to be that first man.

He had always assumed that he would be the first man out of the door when the LM touched down on the lunar surface. In the past, as with the space walks, it had been customary for the commander to remain with the ship while his partner did the moving around.

Then he had learned that Armstrong had decided to exercise his prerogative as commander and would be stepping out of the LM first. There were sound practical reasons for this—Armstrong's position was closest to the door. Even though the logic of this was apparent to a man of Aldrin's intellect, he had still not recovered from the emotional disappointment of being merely the second man to walk on the Moon.

Now all these things seemed like small irritations compared to the UFO business Deke had sprung on them that day at lunch. Against his better judgment, Aldrin allowed himself to dwell on the possibilities. A welcoming party of alien spaceships? He sighed. Perhaps Mike Collins was right. Perhaps the greatest dangers were the ones they had not even prepared for.

Aldrin turned over and drifted off to sleep.

Meanwhile, Collins lay in his bunk, his mind running through the events of the day. Collins was a man with his head in the clouds and his feet firmly on the ground. Some people said that he was the unluckiest member of the Apollo crew because he would miss the glory of the actual Moon walk.

But Mike never saw it that way. He was quite satisfied with his protective role as guardian of the Command Module while his buddies were cavorting around on the Moon far below. Besides, he told himself, there would be other trips, other Moon walks. After playing bridesmaid on this mission, he felt sure that Deke would somehow get him on the flight list for a future voyage to the lunar surface.

In his methodical way, Collins went back over the events of the day. They were going to the Moon, that was the most important thing. All the other stuff, warnings about landings and deadlines and, for God's sake, even UFOs, faded into the background. They were going to the Moon, that was what really mattered. The *Moon*.

Collins fell asleep with a smile on his face. The last image in his mind was of Neil and Buzz cordially inviting two little green men into the LM for coffee and pie.

Armstrong had no trouble sleeping. Despite his years of training and experience, he was in many ways still a farm boy from Wapakoneta, Ohio. He simply rolled over, pulled the covers over his head, and starting snoring. It was not his policy to worry about things he had no control over.

Like Aldrin, Armstrong had got his start as a fighter pilot in the Korean War. After receiving a degree in aeronautical engineering from Purdue, he became a test pilot, flying most of the planes in the U.S. inventory. Soon, his talent got him noticed. It wasn't long before his abilities became legendary.

"Neil doesn't just fly an airplane," one of his fellow pilots said, "he wears it."

Armstrong's uncanny reflexes earned him a great deal of respect from NASA officials when he averted a near-disaster on Gemini 8 while their craft was orbiting the Earth in 1966. A malfunction with one of the rocket thrusters caused the ship to tumble head-over-heels through space.

They were in danger of completely losing control of the craft when Armstrong made the decision to deactivate the flight controls and fire the thrusters manually. He had used up 75 per-cent of the reentry fuel before he regained control of the ship. While the world watched with bated breath, Armstrong fired the retro-rockets and made an emergency splashdown in the Pacific Ocean, miraculously landing just over a mile from the aircraft carrier that had been sent to pick them up.

Needless to say, Deke Slayton and the other NASA officials were highly impressed. They decided that if any American deserved to walk on the Moon, that American was Neil Armstrong.

July 14, 1969

In the last few days before the launch, the dark storm clouds that had been hovering over the Apollo crew mysteriously vanished, and the problems that had bedeviled them for weeks resolved themselves as if by magic. Whatever Slayton and Lovell had done during their brief lunchtime meeting, it had certainly done the trick. The crew was back on track.

On the morning of the 14th, Armstrong made his first successful practice landing of the rocket-powered, free-flight training vehicle at Ellington Air Force Base in Houston. He repeated the landing drill eight times in a row. Thanks to his success in landing the "flying bedstead," he was confident that he could set the LM down sweetly on the Moon.

The preflight frenzy left them no time to worry about little green men. But it did provide them with an illustrious dinner invitation. President Nixon, a great supporter of the Apollo Mission, had asked the astronauts to have a meal with him in their crew quarters the night before the flight. It was a great honor.

But the NASA medical officials wouldn't allow it, fearing that the crewmen might catch a cold from the President. NASA sent regrets. Nixon responded by inviting the pilots and their wives to dinner on their return to Earth. For a President embroiled in an unpopular war in Vietnam and a near-revolution in the streets, the flight to the Moon must have seemed like a rare bright spot in an otherwise dismal era.

As a safeguard against last-minute illness, the crew had been put into quarantine for a week before the flight. NASA Medical Director Charles Berry even made the astronauts wear gas masks when they appeared in public for their final preflight press conferences—a precaution that the pilots regarded as something of a joke.

July 16, 1969

Slayton tumbled the crew out of their beds at 4 A.M. First they were off to breakfast, then for a brief medical checkup, then the complicated ordeal of suiting up. By 6:30, the crew were taking the elevator up to the Command Module, an enclosure shaped like a blunt cone, poised on top of the rocket. This six-ton module, about

10 feet tall and 12 feet across the base, was the only part of the whole assembly that was to make the entire trip. It was a masterpiece of advanced technology packed into the smallest possible space.

The crew's quarters were scarcely bigger than the inside of a station wagon. The astronauts were to lie side by side on seats that were tilted back like couches, cushioned to absorb the impact of a hard landing. The three men grunted with effort as, wearing their bulky flight suits, they slowly wormed their way into position—Collins on the right, Aldrin in the center, Armstrong on the left. Over their faces was the instrument panel, packed with gauges and switches. Five round windows gave them a view of the outside world.

Below Aldrin's feet was the lower equipment bay, where the navigational instruments and other essentials were stored. This would also serve as the entrance tunnel to the LM, which would ride cozily in the body of the third-stage rocket. This semiprivate tunnel would also be where the astronauts would go to relieve themselves.

The inner walls of the CM were battleship gray in color and looked new and shiny. Squares of Velcro decorated the surfaces. These would provide a handy way of attaching things that might float around the cabin in zero-gravity once the craft went into orbit.

By Armstrong's left knee was the abort handle. If things went wrong during blast-off, Armstrong could rotate the handle and the CM rockets would fire, blasting it free from the main rocket and setting the crew down safely by parachute near the launch site.

As they settled into their couches, Collins noticed that the outer leg pocket of Armstrong's suit, designed to hold Moon rocks, was in danger of getting caught on the handle and tripping it accidentally.

When Collins pointed it out, the commander nodded.

"That wouldn't be good," he said, carefully pulling the material away from the handle.

In the early morning light, the *Saturn V* rocket, destined to take them to outer space, looked like an enormous, fire-breathing, steam-venting monster. Taller than a football field set on end, it stood shiny and new against the scarred steel scaffolding of the launch tower.

After running through a checklist of 417 items, the astronauts were ready to slip the bonds of Earth and head for the Moon. They were strapped into their seats by backup crew member Fred Haise. Then the hatch was closed behind them.

Meanwhile, hundreds of miles away, at Mission Control in Houston, Deke Slayton watched the image of the rocket on the television screen in front of him. He and Flight Director Gene Kranz, along with a roomful of NASA technicians, would serve as ground control for the flight.

These operations took place in a 60-by-60 foot room in what came to be called "Building 30." This was Mission Control. The room was laid out like a large auditorium.

In the rear was a 75-seat viewing room. This was where Slayton stationed himself. He didn't want to be in the way. On the other hand, he wanted to be accessible, just in case he should be needed. As it turned out, he was to spend most of the time answering questions from the VIPs who came to the room for a privileged glimpse at the inner workings of the Space Program.

Display screens on the front wall allowed the staff to monitor critical phases of the operation. The largest screen, 18 feet long and 12 feet high, displayed a world map that would later be changed to a map of the path the crew would take through space.

Beneath these displays were four rows of television screens, ten screens to a row. It was here that about 50 technicians, young men in white shirts and black ties, with headsets and microphones poised at their mouths, would wait to monitor the workings of the spacecraft.

For all of its importance, it was not a very comfortable room to work in. The screens were black and white, had poor resolution, and were hard on the eyes. The constant drone of conversation in the controllers' headsets often affected their hearing. But these were discomforts they willingly put up with in exchange for the chance to have a hand in sending a man to the Moon.

The fourth row was the least important, handling mostly minor functions, but the sense of urgency and activity became more intense as you moved forward.

The third row held Flight Director Gene Kranz and the network controller. Kranz was another pilot who had flown in the Korean

War. He had a voice like a Marine drill sergeant and wasn't afraid to use it. When he barked orders, people moved. This was where the critical decisions were made.

In the second row was the Spacecraft Communicator. For the landing phase of the operation, this would be Charlie Duke, a tall, drawling, North Carolinian who had become an astronaut two years before. The communicator was always an astronaut himself and was the one who talked directly to the crew. He was the link between the people on the ground and the people in space.

Although Duke had not yet flown in space, he had trained extensively and knew the astronauts' routines inside out. He had served as communicator for the Apollo 10 mission the year before and had so impressed Armstrong that the commander had personally requested that he serve as communicator for the critical landing phase of the lunar mission.

The guidance, navigation and life support systems also occupied the second row. The men who operated these were known as the 'systems guys'. Their job was to keep watch over the vast and complicated technology which was needed to run the mission.

The front row was referred to as the 'Trench'. Here were stationed the 'trajectory guys', the men who monitored the flight of the craft. It was also the base for the navigator, who monitored the exact position of the spacecraft and made sure that the astronauts were going where they wanted to go.

These technicians bore an immense responsibility. The astronauts might be in control of the craft, but the controllers were in command of the mission. Each set of eyes scanning the screen had to be able to recognize a problem, relay it to the appropriate person and then go on to correct the situation. And they had to be prepared to do it instantly, for hours on end. There were four shifts of six hours each.

Flight Director Gene Kranz was a bit superstitious. For good luck, he always wore a white vest. In a room where most of the men were dressed in nondescript white shirts with narrow black ties, he stood out. He had to. The brunt of the moment-to-moment decisions on this mission would fall on his shoulders. People had to listen to what he said and respond instantly.

After the seemingly endless series of checks and re-checks had been made, there was a long silence. Then the voice of Flight Director Kranz came through the technician's headsets: "Okay, all flight controllers, 30 seconds to ignition."

The adrenaline began to flow in Building 30.

Meanwhile, up in the Command Module, Collins, Aldrin, and Armstrong did their best to relax. As they heard the countdown begin through their headsets, each silently said the astronauts' liftoff prayer: "It won't fail because of me...it won't fail because of me..it won't fail because of me."

Down in the Trench, one of the technicians started the countdown to zero.

"T-minus ten, nine..."

At nine seconds before liftoff, the five gigantic first-stage engines ignited. To the three men, it felt like the rumbling of a volcano in the Earth far below them.

"...eight, seven, six, five..."

The rocket began to vibrate violently.

"... four, three, two, one...Liftoff! We have liftoff!"

The roar of the engines was deafening. As the *Saturn* surged upward at a rate of 88,000 feet per second, the pilots were thrown from right to left, jolting against their harness straps. The first ten seconds were the most dangerous. Then, suddenly, they were clear of the launch tower and on their way. The surging, shuddering *Saturn* settled down and burned clean and strong, roaring over the beaches of Florida, on its way to the Moon. It was 9:35 A.M., Eastern Standard Time.

Back at Mission Control, the room was filled with cheers. Men wiped sweat from their faces and slapped each other on the back. Some lit congratulatory cigars. It had been a perfect liftoff!

The astronauts couldn't hear their cheers. They were already leaving the atmosphere of their home planet and traveling on into the thin void of space.

Right on schedule, the first stage of the *Saturn* rocket burned out and fell away. The second stage carried them 100 miles above the Earth's surface in a mere nine minutes. Then it shut down, again right on schedule, and they were in orbit around the planet Earth. It was 11 minutes from liftoff.

"Shut down," Armstrong said quietly. All was calm and serene.

In zero-gravity now, loose objects began to float around in the capsule. Pens, notebooks, the Hasselblad movie camera, all began to dance around in the CM.

For the first few moments, Collins, Aldrin, and Armstrong moved slowly and deliberately as their bodies adjusted to the new sense of weightlessness. Each of the men was battling with what the training manuals referred to as "stomach awareness," in other words, the desire to be sick. They wanted to avoid this if at all possible; in a zero-gravity environment, there would be no way to contain the vomit and it would float around freely in the cabin for the rest of the voyage.

So far so good. They had survived the first of the ten critical steps on Collins's list. Now they had to get on with the essential task of preparing the CM for its active role as a space vehicle. From here on, it was to be their world.

The astronauts completed their chores in silence. Then, when the first flurry of activities was over, they unzipped their flight suits, took off their helmets and began to make themselves at home. One of the first things they did was to allow themselves a few moments to sit and simply enjoy the view.

Outside their window, the Earth floated like a blue and green beach ball. On its ocean surface, they saw the islands of Bermuda and the Canaries strung out like the beads of a necklace. Collins grinned. He realized then that all the maps he had seen in his life were just a pale representation of what the planet *really* looked like. He wished, for a moment, that his children could be there with him, sitting on his lap and peering in wide-eyed wonder at their world below, so precious and blue, tinged with green and turquoise.

In a twinkling the Canaries were behind them, and Madagascar and Australia came into view. The Earth was beginning to look dark now. It was night on this side of the world.

It was exactly one hour after liftoff and the flight was precisely on schedule. As they passed over the dark ocean just south of Hawaii, the Sun came burning up over the horizon, rising with an astonishing speed.

"Holy cow," Neil said, "get a picture of that!"

Just at that moment, the camera came floating by Collins' head. He reached up and grabbed it, training the lens on the unreal beauty of the sunrise below them.

"Are we hooked up yet for transmission on Earth?" he asked.

Armstrong nodded. "Let's give it a whirl."

Suddenly they heard the voice of Bruce McCandless, the space communicator in Houston for this stage of the mission. "Good picture, guys! We've got you transmitting through our Goldstone, California, antenna. That's a beautiful world you've got in your window."

"Roger that," Collins said. "Beautiful!"

After a few minutes, the sightseeing was over and the camera was stowed away. It was time for everyone to devote their full attention to the Trans-Lunar Injection burn that would blast them out of Earth's orbit and set them on the correct trajectory for their flight to the Moon.

This was a critical burn. The CM would have to reach a speed of about 35,000 feet per second in order to escape the pull of Earth's gravity.

Fired by the computers in Houston, the *Saturn* rocket lit right on time and blasted them free of the Earth's embrace and out into space. Five minutes and forty-five seconds, then shutoff and silence.

"Hey, Houston," Neil radioed back, "that *Saturn* gave us a magnificent ride."

"We copy, Apollo," McCandless said, "keep your fingers crossed."

It was then that Aldrin peered out his window and saw a bright object trailing them.

"Hey, fellas," he said, "you'd better have a look at this."

CHAPTER FIVE

Far below, a bright object sparkled in the blue light of space.

"Hmm," Aldrin said, "let's get a look through the 'scope."

Collins handed Aldrin the monocular telescope. Through the magnifying device, Aldrin could make out the shape of the object. He saw that it wasn't just a point of light.

"Seems to have a sort of 'L' shape to it," Aldrin said, handing the monocular to Armstrong.

The commander said nothing. But he did watch the object for a long time before passing the glass back to Collins.

"What should we do, fellas?" Collins asked. His thoughts flew back to the lunchtime talk with Slayton and Lovell.

"Hey, let's not jump to any conclusions," Aldrin said reasonably. "How far would you say that object is from us?"

Collins fitted his eye to the piece again. "About 100 miles," he answered.

"What's our altitude?"

Collins checked his gauges. "We're about 1,200 miles above the Earth."

"Let's tell Houston about it," Aldrin said, "and find out how far away the third stage of the *Saturn* is at this point."

He was about to reach for the radio switch, when Armstrong touched his arm, stopping him.

"Just a minute, Buzz," Armstrong said. "You're right, let's not jump to any conclusions. Let's not mention anything about this object just yet. Why don't you just ask, in a casual way, how far away our third-stage rocket is at this point?"

Aldrin nodded.

"Houston, this is Columbia."

"Read you, Columbia. Go." It was the familiar voice of Charlie Duke.

"How far away is our *Saturn* third stage right now?"

"I'll check and get back to you."

"Thank you very much."

A moment later, Duke was back on the line.

"Buzz?"

"Yes?"

"Best information we have is that the rocket is about 6,200 miles behind you."

"Thanks, Charlie. No further questions at this time."

"Okay. Keep warm, guys. Give a call if you need anything."

Aldrin turned to the others—Collins looked shaken up. "Let's watch it for a while and see what happens. I don't want to go and report a UFO now. Let's keep an eye on it."

The bright shape was clearly visible for an hour or so before they lost sight of it.

"It was probably one of the discarded panels from our rocket," Armstrong said.

"Yeah," Aldrin muttered. But he didn't sound convinced.

As they left the gravitational pull of Earth, the craft was captured by the gravity of the Moon, and their ship was drawn to the lunar object like an iron ball to a magnet. This journey would take three days.

The crew now entered that strange region between Earth and Moon that is known as Cislunar space. The Earth seemed to be shrinking now—it barely filled one window of the craft. A vague sense of melancholy settled over all three men as they watched their world fade into the background of stars.

Then it was time to sleep. The first night in space.

The crew slept in mesh hammocks strung up in the CM. Because they were in zero-gravity, these hammocks did not hang like the ordinary variety do. They simply kept the men from floating around as they slept. The three astronauts fell asleep without the familiar pressure of mattress, pillow, and bedcovers.

It was a strange sleep that first night, a sleep that gave way to dreams.

Collins dreamed that on a future flight, NASA allowed him to take his six-year-old son along with him. In the midst of the wonderful journey, they stopped long enough on the lunar surface to collect a box of Moon rocks.

Aldrin dreamed as well. He dreamed that he was floating around on the surface of the Moon, almost as easily as he had on the space walks. He was sharply aware that even though the total of his body weight, pressure suit, and life-support backpack would be 350 pounds on Earth, on the Moon the whole thing weighed in at a mere 65 pounds. So he was free to cavort about on the lunar surface, making magnificent jumps and huge, kangaroo-like leaps, sailing effortlessly over the Moon dust.

Turning back to look at the LM, he noticed with alarm that the spidery-looking craft was not in sight. Around him was a cold and alien landscape where one dune and crater looked much like another. Fighting down his sense of panic, Buzz hopped from one spot to another, trying to get his bearings, straining to get a glimpse of the familiar craft. But the LM was not in sight. His wild dream was quickly turning into a nightmare.

Speaking into his microphone, he tried to contact Neil, then Mike. But all he heard was a crackling static through his headphones. Terror crept over him as he considered the awful possibility that he might never see the LM again. By now he was sweating heavily, and the glass of his bubblelike helmet had begun to fog. Eventually, after what seemed like hours, he caught sight of a rectangular opening in the side of a dune. He walked toward it, and as he got closer he noticed that it resembled a mine shaft. Peering down into the hole, he saw a dull greenish light coming from the depths of the Moon. His fear had suddenly turned to fascination. Buzz took a few cautious steps toward the mouth of the shaft. Then, with a violent suddenness, the ground collapsed beneath him and he was falling into an impossibly deep crevasse. Far below, at the bottom, he could make out a glowing, greenish light...

Aldrin woke before he hit bottom. He lay awake for a few moments, momentarily confused. Was he home in his own bed in the Houston suburbs? Or was he in his familiar bunk in the astronaut quarters on the Cape? No, he reminded himself. He was on a spaceship, a spaceship heading for the Moon. He wiped a film of sweat from his face and settled back into an uneasy sleep.

As for Armstrong, he did not have any remarkable dreams. He slept like a farm boy, nestled in the hayloft of a barn.

"Apollo 11, Apollo 11, this is Houston, over."

The voice of Mission Control was insistent, coming through the headset taped to Collins' left ear.

Collins shook himself awake.

"Good morning, Houston," Collins said sleepily, "Apollo 11,

here. Go ahead."

"Good morning. When you are ready to copy, I've got a couple of small flight plan updates for you."

Collins reached for a pad and pen.

"Man," he thought, "not even a cup of coffee to start the day."

He uncapped his pen and began taking down the instructions he was given.

Day two in space had begun.

The Earth was 130,000 miles away. They were nearly halfway to the Moon.

After his morning check-in with Houston, Collins used the hot water spigot to make a plastic bagful of instant coffee. Drinking lousy instant coffee in a plastic bag through a straw wasn't his idea of the best way to start the day. But since there wasn't a diner within 130,000 miles, he reasoned he would have to make do with what he had.

It was while he was sipping his coffee that Collins noticed that a strange change had come over the faces of his crewmates since the night before. Their eyes were closed in sleep as they snoozed away in their hammocks, but Collins had the eerie feeling that they were not the Buzz and Neil he knew. There was something peculiarly different about them, but for a while he couldn't quite make out what it was.

Suddenly, he realized what had happened. With no gravity to pull down the fatty tissue around the eyes, their usually angular faces had become rounded—in fact, almost oriental-looking.

Neil and Buzz woke up to find Mike chuckling to himself. They couldn't figure out why, but at this hour, before they had had their morning coffee, they didn't really care.

The crew spent a very quiet day as the CM was drawn, as if by some magical magnet, to the Moon. Aldrin crawled down through the equipment tunnel and "swam" his way into the LM, which was about the size of two telephone booths put together, to prepare it for the lunar landing on day four.

The LM, or the "Eagle," as Armstrong and Aldrin liked to call it, was a marvel of featherweight technology. Despite its amazing power—its rockets could accelerate from zero to 3,000 miles per hour in less than two minutes—it was surprisingly frail. Everything about it had been constructed to save weight. The fabric walls were so thin that you could easily jab a screwdriver through them. On Earth, the craft wouldn't even support its own weight—it would instantly collapse into a piece of scrap metal.

All the equipment had been stripped down to the minimum. Even the safety covers had been removed from the circuit breakers and switches. So the inner walls of the LM showed miles of exposed wire and plumbing. There were switches and gauges everywhere. The designers had not even put in a seat for the pilot. Armstrong would fly the craft standing up, like a charioteer. He and Aldrin would be held in place with harnesses attached to the floor and ceiling.

From the time they began their descent from the CM, the computer system would fly the craft to a landing, but Armstrong knew that he had to be prepared to take over at any moment. He would make the necessary adjustments with a series of toggle switches. If things went wrong, he could hit the abort handle and powerful rockets would kick in, thrusting them back up into orbit around the Moon where, it was hoped, they could rendezvous with Collins in the CM.

The actual landing would require close teamwork between Aldrin and Armstrong. Just as they had practiced so many times in the simulator, Aldrin would be watching the gauges while Armstrong piloted the LM to touchdown on the Moon.

Because of the hectic work schedule, Aldrin's internal conflict about the Moon walk had stayed pretty much in the background. But now, as the time for the lunar excursion drew near, Buzz once more began to turn the matter over in his mind. He thought briefly of the dream he had had the night before—then he let it go and turned his mind back to more practical matters. No, he told himself firmly, he wasn't worried about being lost on the surface of the Moon. He was just worried about being lost in the pages of history. Buzz realized it was something he would just have to come to terms with, but it wasn't going to be easy.

"By the way," Aldrin asked Armstrong when he had returned from the LM, "when you step out onto the lunar surface, whatever you say is sure to go down in the history books. Have you decided what it'll be?"

Armstrong was eating chicken salad out of a plastic bag.

"Not yet," he said, "I'm still thinking it over."

Aldrin remembered that in the weeks before the flight, there had been a lot of talk on the Cape about what Armstrong should say. Some people had even suggested that NASA had ordered the commander to deliver a scripted message to the public. Finally, the head of the NASA Public Relations Department had got fed up with the whole thing and sent out a memo that essentially said: "Queen Isabella didn't tell Columbus what to say when he landed in the New World. Leave Neil the heck alone."

So, on the eve of the lunar walk, only Armstrong knew what Armstrong would say. And that was the way he wanted it.

CHAPTER SIX

July 19, 1969

The Moon was clearly visible through the windows of the CM. But it wasn't the familiar, romantic disk that love songs are written about. The Moon the astronauts saw now was a monstrously huge sphere, filling the dark sky. Because it was now between the Sun and the CM, the lighting on the lunar surface was spectacular. The Sun, shining from behind it, cast a halo of brilliant light around the rim of the giant ball.

The face of the Moon was illuminated by Earthshine, the Sun's light reflected back from the surface of the Earth. Earthshine on the Moon is considerably brighter than Moonshine on the Earth, making the surface look cool and mysterious.

"It's worth coming just for the view," murmured Armstrong.

For a few moments the crew gazed, spellbound, at this extraordinary sight. Then they were brought back to reality by the voice of Charlie Duke, reminding them that it was time to execute one of the most critical burns of the voyage.

Lunar gravity was pulling them in at a rate of 7,500 feet per second. If they let this process continue, they would crash onto the surface just as countless meteors and other bits of space debris had done every day for the past five billion years.

To avoid this, they would have to follow an exacting path, flying past the Moon, then slowing themselves down enough to be captured by lunar gravity, which would pull them into an elliptical orbit around the mysterious sphere. In precise terms, this meant flying within 300 miles of the surface of the Moon. This was all the more difficult because the Moon is not just a ball hanging in the sky, it is a rotating, moving world, itself orbiting around the Earth, which is, in turn, orbiting around the Sun, which is drifting through space as only a small particle in an ever-expanding galaxy.

Collins checked and rechecked the calculations for the burn, knowing that if they made a mistake, they could blast themselves out of the orbit of the Moon and into the gravitational field of the Sun. If this disaster happened, the CM would become a lump of space junk, permanently orbiting the Sun.

The moment had come. "Here we go, guys," Collins said. He could feel the tension in his voice, but he swallowed hard and carried on.

He flicked a switch, firing the CM rockets. They burned, fierce and strong, for a full six minutes. When they finally shut down, Charlie's voice came crackling triumphantly over the radio:

"Congratulations, fellas. That was a beautiful burn! The computer shows a velocity error of only one-tenth of a mile. You are in orbit!"

In the background, Collins could hear the cheers of their comrades back at Mission Control. He looked over at his crewmates. They grinned back at him. They were now within striking distance of their lunar dreams.

One more precise burn dropped them down to a circular orbit, a mere 60 miles above the surface.

"It looks just like the pictures," Armstrong reported to Houston. "But it's like the difference between watching a real football game and seeing it on TV. There is no substitute for actually being here."

Nobody argued with that.

They could now make out the geographic features quite clearly. They saw places that they had studied on their maps for months: Mount Marilyn (named after Jim Lovell's wife), Duke Island (named after Charlie Duke), Boot Hill, Diamondback, and Sidewinder. Under these lighting conditions, the ridges of the craters cast long, jagged shadows, making the terrain look stark and formidable.

Then, all at once, their landing site on the edge of the Sea of Tranquillity came into view.

"It looks as rough as a corncob down there," Collins said.

It certainly did.

Nobody said anything, but they were all thinking the same thing. How, each of them wondered, are we going to land this frail little LM in the midst of that craggy rock pile?

For the rest of the day their craft spun over the pockmarked surface of this alien world. Late that evening, they settled into their mesh hammocks.

Collins glanced at his watch. It was almost midnight back in Houston. It had been a long and exhilarating day, he mused. But it was nothing compared to how tomorrow would be. Tomorrow would make this day look like a walk in the park. Tomorrow, God willing, his buddies would walk on the Moon.

July 20, 1969

"Apollo 11, Apollo 11, this is the Black Team."

"You guys wake up early," Collins said grumpily into his microphone.

Charlie chuckled. "Looks like you guys were really snoring."

"Didn't sleep very well," Collins admitted. "Only got about five hours shut-eye last night."

"Come on, big guy," Duke said encouragingly, "today's the big day. Wake up and smell the coffee."

Collins groaned inwardly as he thought of the lousy instant coffee.

Buzz and Neil woke up and began moving around, stowing their sleeping gear and getting ready for what would be the biggest day of their lives.

There were hundreds of things to do, and they all needed to be done at once. They had a quick breakfast, then set to work. While Collins got the CM ready, Aldrin and Armstrong prepared to get suited up and crawl into the LM.

Buzz and Neil took a long time getting all the zippers secured and the rings locked into place. They worked slowly and carefully —their lives depended upon these suits. At last they were ready. They waved good-bye to Collins and floated down the tunnel and into the LM. As Mike closed the hatch behind them, the thought suddenly came to him that it might possibly be the last time he ever saw his companions. He quickly cast the idea out of his mind —it was too awful to contemplate.

"Can you hear me, Mike?" Buzz said from the LM.

Collins adjusted his headset.

"Roger that."

"It's going to take us a few minutes to get ready for undocking."

"No sweat. I can hold all day. Just take your own sweet time." Then he added: "Hey, Neil, You're very quiet. Are you okay?"

"No problem," Armstrong said confidently. He was concentrating intently on checking the 600 separate switches that studded the interior walls of the LM.

"Listen," Mike said as sort of a formal good-bye, "you guys take it easy down there."

"Roger that," Buzz said. "We're ready for undocking."

Collins threw the release switch, activating a set of explosives that blasted the LM away from the CM.

In the silence of the lunar void, the "Eagle" spun gracefully away, extending its four spidery landing legs, looking like a giant insect bursting from its cocoon.

"The Eagle has wings!" Buzz cried.

"I'm getting out of the way," Collins radioed back. He fired his thrusters and moved a safe distance away. He could now see the LM through his window. To his eyes, too, it looked like a bizarre flying insect.

"Okay, Mike," Armstrong said, "I'm heading down."

"You guys take care..." Collins said.

"See you later," Armstrong promised. Then he fired his descent engine in a braking burn. They were moving at about 3,000 miles an hour, plunging feet first toward the pockmarked surface of the Moon.

They were due at the Sea of Tranquillity in 12 minutes.

But something was wrong. Armstrong noticed the crater named Maskelyne W flash by their window two seconds sooner than it should have. This might not sound like much of a miscalculation, but at that speed, a two-second error could land the LM 2 miles off course.

"We're coming in a little long," Neil remarked in a matter-of-fact voice.

"Roger, we confirm," Charlie said coolly.

The casual tone of their words betrayed no emotions, but it was apparent to everyone that things were rapidly going wrong. If the velocity of the craft increased by only another 8 miles per hour, the flight plan called for Neil to hit the abort handle and blast back up to the CM. They were coming in too fast.

The decision about what to do next rested on the shoulders of a 30-year-old computer specialist named Steve Bales who sat in the Trench back at Mission Control. He was guidance officer for this critical phase of the operation.

The back of Gene Kranz's lucky T-shirt was soaked with sweat.

"What do you say, Steve?" he asked.

"Give me a minute," Bales said, his eyes scanning the data on the screen in front of him.

"We don't have a minute," Kranz snapped, "I want a decision now."

"I think we're going to make it," Bales said. Then he added weakly, "I think."

"Well," Kranz demanded. "Are we or *aren't* we?"

"We are," he said. This time his voice was more confident.

Bales was right. They did make it. Five minutes into the burn, with the LM plummeting to within 20,000 feet of the Moon, the thrusters did their job, slowing the craft down to an acceptable speed.

"Good," Kranz thought with relief. "We are not going to crash this baby." Relief flooded over him.

But the relief wasn't to last long. At the controls of the speeding LM, Buzz and Neil had new problems.

The LM's on-board computer flashed a warning signal.

"Program alarm," Aldrin said sharply. "It's a 1202."

Bales broke into a cold sweat. This was the computer's way of saying that too much information was coming in too fast and that it would have to shut down until it could catch up with itself.

"Not *now*," Bales groaned in desperation.

"What was that, Steve?" It was Kranz's voice, as harsh as an electric saw in his ear.

"The computer is being overloaded," he explained.

"I know that," Kranz barked back, "what I want to know is— should we abort?"

Bales took a deep breath. His response was based purely on instinct. "No, go ahead."

"Go ahead? With the computer down?"

Bales turned around in the Trench and stared at Krantz.

"Look," he said, "who are you going to believe, me or some computer? I think it will clear itself."

Kranz smiled at the young man's self-assurance. Then he turned back to the microphone.

"You are GO for landing," he said.

"That's what we want to hear," Aldrin said. After coming so close, the thought of having to abort was almost unbearable.

At eight minutes into the powered descent, the LM was at 6,800 feet, traveling at a rate of 60 miles per hour. According to the flight plan, Armstrong had to touch down within six minutes or hit the abort handle.

Because of the faltering computer, Armstrong decided to fly the craft in manually. He grasped the red-colored pistol grip on his right and placed his finger on the thruster toggle switch on his left.

At 2,460 feet, the computer flashed a second warning.

"1201," Aldrin barked.

"1201," Armstrong repeated.

As Armstrong watched his gauges he saw that the computer problems were causing the LM to overshoot the landing site by as much as four miles.

In the meantime, the surface of the Moon was rushing up fast.

At an altitude of 1,000 feet, Armstrong saw that they were descending toward a crater filled with a jumble of jagged boulders. He knew the frail LM could not possibly survive a landing there.

While Armstrong guided the craft in, Aldrin kept his eyes on the gauges, calling out the altitude and velocity readings in a steady, reliable drone. The teamwork they had developed during those weeks in the simulator was paying off. They had practiced this hundreds of times. Now it was for real.

"Six hundred and eighty-five feet, twenty feet per second..."

"Five hundred and ninety feet, down to 18 feet per second..."

They were now almost four miles off course and running dangerously low on fuel. Armstrong was painfully aware that the Moon was one place where he couldn't let his fuel tank go dry looking for a parking space. If that happened, they would have no way of firing the ascent engine, and they would be stranded on the surface of the Moon forever. They would die there.

At only 200 feet above the lunar surface, Armstrong finally sighted a level spot, free from boulders, where he thought he could set the LM down safely.

"Sixty seconds of fuel remaining," Charlie said over the radio.

Armstrong jerked the LM into an upright landing position and began to set her down. The descent engines kicked up a cloud of Moon dust.

"Thirty seconds of fuel," Duke reported.

Neil knew that they needed 20 seconds of fuel to blast back up to the CM. He was cutting it awfully fine.

"Forty feet," Aldrin said. "We're kicking up some dust."

Back in the Trench, Steve Bales had already begun the countdown to abort. But it was too late. The astronauts were already in the "dead man's zone."

"What do you say, Steve?" It was Kranz's voice again.

"We're GO!" Bales said.

"You are GO for landing," Charlie echoed.

Duke started to call out another fuel reading, but he was interrupted by the presence of a man who had been watching from the control booth for days, a man who had now come out into the operations room. Deke Slayton had moved up and taken the seat beside him at the console.

"Shut up, Charlie," Slayton ordered. "Let them land."

Everyone in Building 30 held their breath as Neil drifted the LM down through the "dead man's zone."

He set it down so sweetly that Aldrin had to look at the contact light to make sure they were on the ground. He checked his gauges. They had 20 seconds of fuel remaining.

"Contact light!" Aldrin said triumphantly.

"We copy you down, Eagle," Charlie Duke said.

"Houston, Tranquillity Base here," Armstrong announced. "The Eagle has landed."

"Roger, Tranquillity, we copy you on the ground. We've got a bunch of guys just about to turn blue here. Now we can all breathe again. Thanks a lot." The relief in Charlie's voice was obvious.

The guys in Building 30 certainly were breathing again. With the tension of the Moon landing over, they all began talking at once.

But Kranz cut through the chatter.

"Knock it off!" he yelled. "Get back to your consoles! Those guys need us to be keeping an eye on things."

Meanwhile, up in the CM, Collins had missed the whole thing. He was orbiting on the dark side of the Moon and was out of communication. He wouldn't learn the good news until the Eagle had already been safely landed for several minutes.

Down on the Moon, the dust was settling around the LM. Armstrong turned to Aldrin and, wordlessly, they shook hands. They had made it.

Despite his achievement in landing the LM safely, Armstrong, ever the perfectionist, felt compelled to apologize for his lengthy landing procedure.

"Houston," he radioed back, "that must have seemed like a very long final phase. The computer was taking us into a place about the size of a football field, filled with large boulders. So I had to find a better parking spot."

"Roger," Duke said. "Sounds good to us, Tranquillity. Be advised that there are a lot of smiling faces in this room right now."

"And two of them up here," Aldrin said.

Suddenly the voice of Collins joined in, as the CM reappeared from the dark side of the Moon.

"And don't forget one in the Command Module," he said. "You guys did a fantastic job."

"It was really rough, Mike," Armstrong confided. "Extremely rough landing spot."

"When in doubt," Collins said, "land long."

Armstrong smiled.

"So we did."

But "landing long" had created a new problem for the guys in the Trench. Because Armstrong had not used the proposed landing site, no was really sure where they were.

"Houston, this area doesn't look familiar to me," Aldrin said. "I haven't even been able to get a good look out the windows yet."

"Roger, Tranquillity. No sweat. We'll figure it out."

Then Aldrin did have a chance to look out the window.

"Hey, Neil," he said, "you'd better come and have a look at this."

CHAPTER SEVEN

Armstrong bent and squinted through the LM window. He now had a chance to take a more careful look at the landing site he had chosen so hastily a few moments before. It was a flat area, about the size of a small house and yard, bordered on the right by two massive craters and on the left by a pile of car-sized boulders.

Almost right away he noticed a reddish, throbbing light coming from the boulder pile. Then, as he looked more closely among the rounded forms of the Moon rocks, he could make out the outlines of a large, angular object, sitting back in the shadows, like a giant bird on its nest.

"Buzz?" Armstrong said. His voice was just a whisper in the quiet of the LM. "Buzz, what do you think that is?"

Aldrin was staring at the strange object too. He was absolutely speechless. "It could be some kind of reflection, right?" Armstrong continued. "Maybe it's our own lights, shining off the rocks there —*Buzz*?"

At last Aldrin tore his eyes away from the windows and muttered into his microphone, "Houston, be advised—There is a Santa Claus."

Down at Mission Control, Gene Kranz motioned to his communications officer.

"Get them off-line, *now!*"

A half a billion people, glued to their TV sets all over the world, were surprised when the thrilling news account of the lunar landing was suddenly cut short. As commentators scrambled to maintain their poise in front of the cameras, and network executives shouted into their telephones, Kranz laid down the word to the men in Building 30.

"Keep those media people off my back until we figure this out," he ordered.

Bruce McCandless was on shift again now as the communicator. Deke Slayton, seated nearby, leaned into Bruce's microphone.

"Eagle," he said, "this is Deke. Do you read me?"

"Roger, Houston," Aldrin said.

Armstrong still hadn't taken his eyes off the pulsing light.

"What have you got, Buzz?" Slayton said.

"Am I off-line?"

"That's affirmative. Give us a report."

"Well, Deke—How can I say this? We've got a strange kind of light here, about—it's hard to tell—about 600 feet away?"

Armstrong shook his head. "Closer than that—I'd say about 450."

"Yeah, I guess that's right. We can't really make out the form of this thing—all we can see is an outline..."

"An outline of what?" Deke demanded.

"Heck, I don't know. I guess you could say it looks like a..."

There was a long silence.

"Buzz?"

"I'm here, Deke."

"Well, spit it out, boy, what does it look like?"

"Well—it looks like a ship."

"Say that again?"

Armstrong broke in. "Deke, I know this is hard to believe, but this thing does not appear to be part of the moonscape. It is giving off a reddish, pulsing light at three or four second intervals. Deke—I'm sure there is a logical explanation for this..."

"Listen gentlemen," Deke's voice cut in, "I need answers and I need them right now. First of all: Do you detect any hostile intent?"

"No," Aldrin put in, "whatever it is just sits there—as if it's watching us."

"You're sure?"

"No, of course I'm not sure!" Aldrin said irritably. He was beginning to realize the full impact of the fact that they weren't the first living beings to land on the Moon. And Houston could do nothing to help them.

"Okay, Buzz, okay. I hear you." Slayton spoke soothingly. Hold tight, buddy. I'll get an advisory from the Trench and we'll blast you guys out of there."

"No," Buzz said tensely. "I don't think that's advisable. Any sudden action on our part could be provocative. Let's just sit tight and see what happens."

Slayton was silent for a moment, then leaned into the microphone. "We copy. Sit tight. But be prepared to blast off at a

41

moment's notice."

"Roger," Aldrin said.

But when he glanced over at his crewmate, Buzz saw that Neil had his face pressed to the glass. His eyes were large and luminous and seemed to be filled with the strange light.

"Neil?"

Armstrong didn't answer.

Aldrin reached out and grabbed him by the shoulder.

"Neil? Come on, buddy, we've got work to do." He shook him gently.

Then Armstrong turned, and Buzz could see that the light had penetrated the farm boy's eyes, making them look ghostly and strange.

"I wish I could take a closer look," Armstrong muttered quietly, almost to himself.

Aldrin pulled Neil away from the window.

"Come on, fella, snap out of it!" He spoke sharply. They couldn't afford to lose control now.

Armstrong rubbed his hand across his eyes.

"Sorry," he said, "I guess I kinda got sidetracked there."

When he looked at Aldrin again, the commander's eyes had lost their eerie glimmer. He was his old self again.

"What's the situation?" he asked.

Aldrin sighed.

"I got on the radio and called down to Houston. They advised us to prepare for liftoff. But I think we should sit here for a while and get a better idea of what's really going on."

Just then, Collins voice came crackling over the lines. He was almost lost in static.

"What's going on, fellas? I'm heading over to the other side now, so I'm losing a lot of what you're saying. You got a problem down there?"

"We think there's something down here—maybe a ship," Aldrin said.

A rush of static came over the lines.

"What did you say?" Collins said. "Your transmission is cutting out on me."

"Columbia, can you hear me now?" Aldrin said.

But there was just a rush of static on the line. The CM had

passed on to the dark side of the Moon.

Houston's line, however, was loud and clear. Slayton's voice came through the wires as clearly as a phone call from home.

"Eagle, this is Slayton, is Neil okay?"

"No problem," Armstrong answered. "I'm just a little shaken here, Deke, I've never seen anything quite like this."

Aldrin turned back to the window. He began speaking slowly into his microphone.

"Whatever it is appears to be covered with lights—brilliant lights. It hurts the eyes to look at them for too long."

Aldrin turned away and closed his eyes tightly, trying to drive away the stinging sensation.

"How should we proceed, Houston? I can blast us out of here right now," Armstrong said.

"Hold one minute," Slayton said.

A moment later, he was back on-line.

"Neil, we want you guys to just hold on there. Don't do anything that could be interpreted as an aggressive act. Just keep an eye on things and keep us up to date..."

"That's an affirmative," Armstrong said.

He turned to Aldrin.

"Well, Buzz, we're here for a while. I guess now is the time to get out the coffee cups and the pie plates."

Despite the seriousness of the situation, Aldrin grinned. Good old Neil.

For an hour they waited, occasionally glancing out at the mysterious object nestled among the boulders.

Meanwhile, Kranz put them back on-line, and both Buzz and Neil did their best to make some contact with the broadcast audience. They knew they had to sound as if everything was going according to plan.

Buzz called for a moment of silence.

"I'd like to take this opportunity to ask every person listening in, whoever and wherever they may be, to pause for a moment and contemplate the events of the past few hours and give thanks in his or her own way."

Later, Armstrong gave the audience a careful description of the scene outside his window—with one important omission.

He said nothing about the eerie object or the strange, pulsing light.

"The sky is black, you know. A very dark sky. But the surface looks kind of warm and inviting. It looks like it would be a nice place to take a sunbath. You feel like going out there in nothing but a bathing suit to get a tan."

With their public relations work done, the astronauts settled back into the task of trying to assess their predicament. They were in a situation that no pilot before them had ever encountered.

Again Collins reappeared from the dark side of the Moon, and Armstrong briefed him on the incredible events.

"If this is one of your practical jokes," Collins said, "I don't think it's funny. You guys are really..."

"It's not a joke," Aldrin broke in. "Look, I know it's hard to grasp. I mean, I'm here looking at the thing and it's hard for me to believe. But it's real, Mike. This is really happening."

Collins didn't answer right away. Orbiting around the Moon in the CM, he felt terrified for his partners—and horribly alone.

"All right," he radioed back. "I get the message. If you guys decide to lift off, let me know and I'll do whatever I can to rendezvous with you."

"We copy," Armstrong said. "We'll keep you informed."

Collins signed off.

Meanwhile, in Houston, a heated debate was raging across the consoles in Building 30.

"The pressure from the media is getting pretty intense," Kranz was saying. "The phone lines are jammed with irate press and TV types who want to know what happened to their coverage."

"So *what*?" Slayton shot back. Satisfying the media was the last thing on his mind.

"Listen, Slayton, let me explain something to you." Kranz spoke slowly. "NASA needs the support of the American public to keep the Space Program going. The hardworking citizens of the United States have paid $13 billion to see a man walk on the Moon and, by God, that's what I'm going to give them."

Deke got to his feet and walked up to within a few inches of the flight director. His voice was trembling with suppressed anger.

"You're not putting my boys into a potentially dangerous

situation just for a lousy publicity stunt! Kranz, what's wrong with you? Those men would gladly give their lives to make this mission a success—but I'm not going to sit by and watch them sacrificed just for a stupid TV show!"

"I'm sorry, Deke," Kranz said quietly. "I've got orders from higher up. My hands are tied. I gotta do what I'm told, just like you do. Now if you can't sit in here and help with the effort, I'll have you escorted back to your quarters."

Slayton stared back at him. He couldn't believe what he was hearing.

He opened his mouth to argue—then, over Kranz's shoulder, he saw a knot of NASA top brass watching him through the glass of the viewing room. He was hopelessly outnumbered.

For a brief moment, Slayton almost walked out. But he fought down the impulse as soon as it arose. He knew he wouldn't be any good to his crew if he left the room. He would have to stay even if it meant knuckling under to Kranz. He would do whatever it took to get them through this absurd situation.

"I'll follow orders, all right," Slayton growled, "but I don't have to like it."

"No, you don't," Kranz said firmly.

"Eagle, this is Houston, do you copy?" It was Bruce McCandless' voice coming over the lines.

"This is Eagle, go ahead," Armstrong said.

"Anything happening?"

"No change."

"All right then," McCandless said. "Be advised that you are to begin preparations for the Extra-Vehicular Activities."

Armstrong couldn't believe he had heard right.

"Say that again?"

"Prepare for the Moon walk."

Armstrong and Aldrin cast a long, incredulous glance at each other, then at the throbbing lights outside their window.

"Houston—am I off-line?"

"Roger that."

"Houston, I don't think this is an advisable time to do the EVA, given the special circumstances of our situation." Armstrong spoke slowly, in measured tones.

"We copy, Eagle. Be advised, we have orders to proceed with the Moon walk if at all possible."

Again the astronauts exchanged glances. Then the commander seemed to arrive at some sort of decision. His manner changed to one of brisk efficiency.

"That's an affirmative," he said.

Aldrin shook his head. He had grave doubts about this.

"They can't be serious!"

"You heard them," said Armstrong. He sounded impatient now.

"But, Neil," Aldrin began to protest, "do you honestly think its wise to get close to that...that *thing* out there?"

"Get suited up, Buzz. You wanted so badly to walk on the Moon. Now we're going to do it. The way I look at it, we really don't have much choice. If we lift off, we might provoke a reaction. If we just sit here and stare at each other, our oxygen will run out and we will have to return to the CM without ever knowing what it was like to set foot on another world. The way I see it, if we are in any danger, I'd rather die with my boots on, out there in the Moon dust, than cooped up in this flying telephone booth."

Aldrin stared at Armstrong for a moment in disbelief. Then his face broke into a grin. Buzz recognized that, in a strange sort of way, what his companion was saying made perfect sense.

"All right," he said, "let's go out and get some Moon rocks."

Neil and Buzz put on their pressure suits in wary silence, from time to time throwing glances at the shape that sat, seemingly watching them, at the edge of the landing site.

Getting into the suits took them seven hours. Every zipper and ring had to be painstakingly locked into place. The astronauts were aware that the slightest exposure to the Moon's natural conditions would mean loss of consciousness and death within seconds.

When they were finally suited up, they helped each other on with their backpacks. These portable life-support systems were to provide them with everything they needed during their foray onto the lunar surface. The backpacks gave them a steady flow of clean, filtered oxygen, powered a heating and cooling system, and contained a portable communications unit.

Their final task was to lock on their helmets and gloves.

At last Armstrong said, "Houston, we are ready to proceed with the EVA."

"That's a GO," Bruce said.

"I'm depressurizing the cabin now," Armstrong noted, breathing in the steady flow of air coming from his backpack unit.

"Roger that," Houston answered. "I'm putting you fellas back on-line now. We've got the TV camera on the porch of the LM ready to go. Remember, from now on everything you do and say will be seen and heard by the public, so be careful. If you see any change in the situation up there, just say the code words and we'll take you off-line."

"We copy," Armstrong said.

He opened the hatch and began backing out onto the porch of the LM.

It was 9:30 in the evening, Houston time.

"Okay, Neil," Bruce said, "we can see you coming down the ladder now."

People all over the world saw the fuzzy image of Armstrong moving slowly, awkwardly down the metal rungs, hopping with his feet together, like a kangaroo, from one rung to the next.

"I'm at the foot of the ladder now," he said. He turned to face the pulsing light, which was out of the camera's range. Armstrong wanted desperately to keep watching the light, to wait for something to happen. Instead, he made himself look down at his feet.

"I'm going to step off the LM now."

Over the last few days he had given a great deal of thought to what he was going to say when he set foot on the Moon. But he had not decided exactly how he would word things until he and Buzz were suiting up. After the confusing events of the last few hours, he wondered if the words he had chosen would truly do justice to the enormity of what he was about to do.

It was 9:56 Houston time when Armstrong stepped out of the dish-shaped landing pad and made the first human footprint on the surface of the Moon. All over the world, people watching the ghostly black-and-white image of Armstrong waited to hear his words.

Finally they came.

"That's one small step for man, one giant leap for mankind."

Buzz wrinkled his brow. 'What?' he thought. 'That doesn't

make sense, Neil.'

Then he realized that what Armstrong probably meant to say was: 'That's one small step for a man, one giant leap for mankind.'

But, in the excitement of the moment, being the first man to step onto the Moon in full view of an alien spacecraft and half a billion viewers, Aldrin could hardly blame him for fluffing his line.

Then Armstrong stepped away from the LM. Immediately, the landing site was filled with a sudden, intense burst of reddish light. Armstrong and Aldrin threw back their heads in amazement as, without a sound, the enormous object lifted from the boulder field and shot upward at an incredible speed. In a moment, it was gone, disappearing without trace into the star-studded sky overhead.

The whole thing had happened in the blink of an eye. There was no time to retreat, no time to say "Santa Claus," no time to do anything. And now, for the moment, Neil and Buzz were alone on the Moon.

"Eagle, this is Houston. I've taken you off-line again. What was that flash?"

"It's gone! Whatever it was just took off like a shot!" Armstrong said.

"It happened really fast," Aldrin cut in. "There was no engine thrust, nothing, just a clean, quiet exit."

Deke was back on the line.

"Eagle, this is Slayton. Use your best judgment up there, guys. I don't want you in any more danger than you have to be."

"Roger that," Armstrong said. "From what I could see, I think we're okay now."

"We copy, Neil. But if you see anything strange, head back to the LM."

"Thanks for your concern, Deke. But, just between you and me, if anything happens, it'll probably happen so fast that there won't be anything either you or I can do about it."

"Then head for the LM now. We don't need any dead heroes up there."

"I came here to walk on the Moon," Armstrong said, "and that's what I'm going to do."

"Okay, Buzz," Armstrong said, "we're ready to bring down the camera."

Warily, Aldrin handed the Hasselblad black-and-white movie

camera down to Armstrong. Aldrin backed out of the LM and kangaroo-hopped down the ladder while Neil dutifully filmed his first steps on the Moon. Both were painfully aware that everything they did was being monitored by the people back on Earth. They had to act as if nothing unusual was going on.

But from time to time, they cast a wary eye to the sky, wondering who else was watching.

CHAPTER EIGHT

July 20, 1969

Neil and Buzz sounded almost like tourists as they reported back to Earth, trying to describe what it was like to be on the Moon.

"It has a stark beauty all its own," Armstrong told the broadcast audience. "It's a bit like some of the high desert in the United States. It's different, but it's very pretty out here."

"Magnificent," Aldrin agreed. "Magnificent desolation."

But now there was work to do.

The astronauts would have less than two hours on the surface of the Moon. In that time they had a rigorous schedule of chores, both scientific and diplomatic, to complete.

One of their diplomatic chores was to leave a special inscribed plaque on the Moon. This was attached to the leg of the LM and, as part of the lower landing assembly, would be left behind when the LM lifted back off into space. Armstrong pointed to the plaque as he read out the words to the broadcast audience:

"Here men from the planet Earth

First set foot upon the Moon

July 1969, A.D.

We came in peace for all mankind."

Now, he was beginning to wonder if maybe the message should have been different. Maybe they should have extended their peaceful intent toward *all* forms of life, not just the human ones.

They made a start on the the scientific tasks.

Before doing anything else, Armstrong picked up a handful of Moon dust and put it into the side pocket of his suit. They might just have to lift off unexpectedly, and they didn't want to come all the way to the Moon and then go back without a sample of lunar soil.

Aldrin set up a device for measuring solar wind, while Armstrong set out the rock collection boxes.

Mike Collins, still in orbit around the Moon, heard Bruce McCandless' voice coming over the radio. "I guess you're about the only person around who doesn't have TV coverage of this scene."

"That's all right," he radioed back, "I don't mind a bit. How is the quality of the TV?"

"Oh, it's beautiful. Really is, Mike. They've got the flag up and you can see the Stars and Stripes on the lunar surface."

But getting the flag up had been no easy task. Just beneath the fine, powdery surface, the subsoil was very dense. Buzz and Neil were only able to push the flagpole into the ground a few inches. It wasn't very stable and they didn't want the flag to topple over in front of a half a billion TV viewers.

Also, because there is no wind on the Moon, the designers had thoughtfully included an aluminum arm that could be folded out to keep the flag extended. But the arm malfunctioned and was so short that they had to erect the flag with a permanent wave in it.

"Don't worry about it," Buzz said to Neil, "I think it looks more patriotic that way."

Armstrong took a picture of Aldrin saluting the flag, and they were about to change positions for another photograph, when they heard Bruce's voice coming through their headsets. "Neil and Buzz," he announced, "the President of the United States is in his office and would like to say a few words to you."

"That would be an honor," Armstrong said.

"Go ahead, Mr. President," they heard Bruce say.

"Hello, Neil and Buzz," Nixon began, "I am talking to you from the Oval Office at the White House. And this certainly has to be the most historic phone call ever made. I just can't tell you how proud we all are of you. For one precious moment, all the people of this Earth are truly one. We pray that you return safely to Earth."

As the President spoke, Armstrong wondered whether it was possible that he might have been told about the real circumstances of their visit.

"Thank you, Mr. President," he said. "It's a great honor to be here representing not only the United States but men of peace of all nations—and men with a vision for the future."

For the rest of the Moon walk, they collected rocks and conducted a series of brief experiments. They saw no more signs of UFOs.

At last Aldrin heard Bruce's voice telling them to prepare to return to the LM.

"This is Houston. Be advised, you have approximately three

minutes until you must commence your EVA termination activities."

Buzz sighed. "Roger. Understand."

He felt almost as if they were children, being called in from recess by their teacher. He motioned to Armstrong.

It was hard work getting the boxes, containing 40 pounds of Moon rocks, into the LM. It took a series of clumsy, kangaroo hops for Buzz and Neil to get back up the ladder. To save weight on the liftoff, they left their backpacks, their boots, and a pile of miscellaneous items on the surface. Neil took a last look at the world they had explored and closed the LM hatch.

The cabin was repressurized, and they had just taken off their helmets and gloves when they became aware of a strange smell. They both sniffed.

"Smells like gunpowder, or maybe a kid's cap gun," Neil remarked.

Aldrin looked down at the legs of their spacesuits.

"I'll bet it's this Moon dust," he said, pointing to the powdery, charcoal-black particles sticking to their legs.

"The smell of the Moon," Armstrong mused.

The two men were just beginning to relax after their adventure when Armstrong noticed something that made his heart sink.

"Buzz," he said, trying to sound calm, "would you look around and see if you can find a little piece of red plastic on the floor?"

"Plastic? What for?"

Armstrong swallowed. He gestured toward the back wall of the cabin.

"Look here, the switch that fires the ascent rocket broke off. I guess I must have hit it with my backpack when I was backing out of the hatch."

"That's not good," Buzz said.

He bent down and began scanning the floor, but after examining the switch more closely, Neil stopped him.

"Forget it," he said. "The whole thing is broken off. There's no way to get hold of it."

The enormity of the problem was obvious: If they couldn't fire the ascent rocket, they would have to stay on the Moon.

For a minute or two they both stood, silently turning the problem over in their minds. Then Buzz had a brain wave.

He pulled a felt-tip pen from his pocket.

"Try this," he said.

Armstrong jammed it into the broken switch. He fiddled with it for a moment, then nodded.

"That'll do it!" he said. Neil whistled with relief, but for a few seconds Buzz thought his chest would burst with the rush of tension he had just felt.

It was past 12:30 in the morning, Houston time. The astronauts had been going strong for almost 20 hours. They had every right to be exhausted, and they were. The flight plan called for them to get a night's sleep in the LM then blast back up to meet the orbiting CM in the morning.

There was one small problem. There wasn't room in the LM for both men to lie down. They tried sleeping standing up, but even in this low-gravity environment, it was just not a practical arrangement. Eventually, they devised a way of lying down in the LM. Armstrong used a harness strap to rig up a kind of hammock and Aldrin curled up on the floor. But still, sleep would not come. Because the lunar temperature outside was below zero, the inside of the LM soon grew chilly and uncomfortable. After about three hours it became unbearably cold, and the men felt as if they were freezing to death. Somehow, they shivered through the night, finally dropping off for a few hours in early morning.

Perhaps due to their exhaustion, or because the day's events had been just too momentous to comprehend right away—neither man discussed the Eagle's strange alien encounter.

July 21, 1969

After their miserable night, Neil and Buzz were glad to hear the voice of the commander of the backup crew, Jim Lovell, coming in over the morning communications:

"Eagle and Columbia, this is the backup crew. Our congratulations on yesterday's performance, and our prayers are with you for the rendezvous."

"Thank you very much," Armstrong said.

Astronaut Ron Evans was the new shift communicator in Houston.

"Okay, fellas," he said at about 2:15 Houston time, "let's light that baby up. Mike is waiting for you guys overhead."

"Roger that," Armstrong said.

He and Buzz were strapped into their harnesses, fully dressed, with helmets on and were ready to leave the Moon and its strange adventures behind.

Armstrong pulled down on Buzz's felt-tip pen and the ascent engine roared to life.

As Buzz glanced out the LM window, he saw a cloud of dust kicked up by the engine and caught a fleeting glimpse of the American flag falling over.

The LM engine burned hard and strong for a full seven minutes, carrying them into orbit, 60 miles above the lunar surface. They were now circling the Moon, a mere 250 miles behind the CM.

Meanwhile, Collins was preparing to welcome his comrades back into the CM. Now both the LM and the CM were orbiting the the Moon, it was time to begin the tricky process of bringing the two objects within kissing distance of each other. When this was done, Collins would perform the exacting docking motions that would link the CM and the LM together once again.

His greatest fear was that he would be unable to retrieve the LM from its lunar orbit and that he would have to fly home alone, having failed in his lifesaving mission. He checked and rechecked his calculations.

At last, Mike saw the LM through his window.

"Buzz," he said urgently, "it sure is good to look down there and see you! I figure we're within 90 miles of each other."

"Roger that," Aldrin said chuckling. "Good to be back in the neighborhood. How long until we rendezvous?"

"Coming up in one minute, how am I looking, Neil?"

"Pretty good, we're flying in formation—like a flock of Canada geese," Armstrong said. "I'm going to execute my burn now. We're burning..."

Collins watched as the fragile-looking craft soared upward, into his flight path. For an instant, he was seized by an irrational fear that the two crafts would collide. Then, as quickly as the thought appeared, he swept it away. They had practiced this maneuver in the simulator hundreds of times. There was no reason why it should go wrong now.

Collins began to mutter under his breath, "It won't fail because of me... It won't fail because of me..."

Then, as if by magic, the LM locked into orbit, less than 50 feet in front of the CM.

"Attaboy!" Collins said. "Burn complete!"

"Burn complete," Armstrong said calmly, as if he had just backed his sports car into a tight parking space at the local shopping mall.

Bruce McCandless' voice came crackling over the radio. "Congratulations, boys! Now dock that thing!"

"You ready for a little bump, Neil?" Collins asked.

"Roger that. We're all yours."

Collins looked keenly through his window. The LM hovered, less than ten feet away. Carefully, he lined up the capture latches and fired the gas jet that would bring the two craft together. But just as he hit the button, the LM began to veer away, like a wild horse trying to evade the lasso.

Almost at the same instant, both Mike and Neil fired their directional rockets to correct the angle. There was an agonizing ten or fifteen seconds when the crafts hovered near each other, not quite touching—then the astronauts heard a loud BANG as the 12 capture hatches locked down tight. They were docked!

The months of preparation in those simulators had served them well—they had performed a carefully rehearsed dance in space, almost as if they were reading each other's thoughts.

But Collins didn't waste any time on self-congratulations. What he wanted most was to see his crewmates again, to see with his own eyes that they were alive and well.

Mike opened the hatch and floated up into the LM. The two lunar explorers peered at him from the half-darkness, their eyes glowing and their faces darkened with beard stubble. Collins smiled. It was the same old Buzz and Neil, hardly changed by their hair-raising adventure.

"Good to see you guys again," Collins called out, "I was worried about you down there."

"So were we," Aldrin confided. For a moment he looked serious. Then, brightening, he said. "Hey Mike, come and give us a hand with these boxes of Moon rocks!"

Two 40-pound boxes, shiny metal caskets about two feet long, were passed from hand to hand up from the LM into the CM. For a few moments the three men floated there, marveling at these strange souvenirs from another world. Then the rocks were stowed away safely in zippered bags.

Now that he had his companions back, Collins could hardly stop talking. His 28 hours of solitude in the CM seemed to have made him hungry for conversation. He bombarded Neil and Buzz with questions:

"How was the liftoff from the Moon? What did it feel like? The landing wasn't a problem, was it? Because the dust was firm underneath you? How about the surface of the Moon itself, what color was it?"

Buzz and Neil tried to give answers, but Collins raced on ahead, interrupting them, asking more questions, talking his head off. They felt like schoolboys, just returning from a wild adventure.

Eventually Slayton's voice came in over their headsets, loud and clear.

"Congratulations on an outstanding job. You guys really put on a great show up there. I think it's time you powered down and got some rest. I look forward to seeing you guys when you get back here. Don't fraternize with any of those bugs up there."

"Thank you, boss," Armstrong said. "See you when we get there."

Still reeling from their adventure on the Moon, Armstrong and Aldrin luxuriated in the relative safety and comfort of the CM. Even though they were almost 168,000 miles from home, they felt as if they were back in a familiar environment.

They now had the bittersweet pleasure of releasing the LM. Collins hit the latch release, there was a small bang, and Buzz and Neil watched as their lunar chariot glided off, to circle the Moon forever.

"She was a good ship," Buzz said quietly.

"She sure was," Armstrong agreed.

"I'm glad to see it go," Collins confided. "Let's head for home!"

Armstrong and Aldrin fairly glowed. Their mission, despite many setbacks and a few near-disasters, had been an unqualified success. Now it seemed that the hardest part was behind them. All they had to do was point their noses at that beautiful green and blue planet and do what the NASA guidebook called a Trans-Earth Injection. The astronauts themselves called it something else. To them it was the "get-us-home-we-don't-want-to-be-a-permanent-satellite-of-the-Moon" burn.

To do it, Collins had to fire their one and only engine for two and half minutes, flinging them from their orbit on the dark side of the Moon into an exacting trajectory that would carry them back to Earth. Despite all the fine numerical calculations, Collins fervently hoped that they would be pointed in the right direction—otherwise they would be veering off into deep space, with no way of turning back.

Right on schedule, Collins executed the burn that would free them from their lunar orbit. Houston, thoughtful as ever, notified them of the exact moment when they were free of the Moon's influence. The gravity of Earth had reclaimed them and was now drawing them home.

"God bless Sir Isaac Newton," whispered Collins.

Shortly afterward, he noticed that his crewmates were beginning to droop. They answered his questions with less and less enthusiasm. Buzz Aldrin and Neil Armstrong, had not slept in over 20 hours, and now they were fading fast. Soon they curled up in their hammocks and dropped off into a deep slumber. Collins sat at the controls, smiling to himself, happy as a mother hen with all her chicks back in the nest, safe and sound.

July 24, 1969

"It has been done before," Collins told himself. "We will do it again."

But now, with less than an hour before they reentered the Earth's atmosphere, he was painfully aware that many things would have to go exactly as planned for the CM to splashdown safely in the Pacific.

"Whatever you do," Houston's Ron Evans had joked, "be sure you guys come in blunt end forward."

"Don't be a wise guy," Collins radioed back.

Blunt end forward was the only way they *could* come in—unless the pointed heat shield was facing forward, the tremendous temperature from the friction created by their reentry to the

Earth's atmosphere would literally burn them up.

"You're cleared for landing," Evans said at last.

"We appreciate it, Ron" Collins said. "We're going into reentry now."

"Roger that, talk to you on the other side," Houston replied.

This simple exchange was actually loaded with meaning. During the ship's reentry, there would be a communication blackout for approximately three minutes. This would be precisely at the time when the heat of the reentry would be at its most intense. If there were any cracks in the heat shield, the astronauts would be incinerated within seconds. All Houston would hear during the final moments of reentry would be a deathly silence.

All three members of the Apollo crew knew that this last phase of the operation was a difficult one, one which would mean the difference between a triumphant success and a disastrous failure.

Now, when Collins glanced out his window, he could see a change. The blackness of space was gone. The first reaches of Earthly light were coloring the sky, and the vast surface of the Earth, with its gently curving horizon, was visible through the window. Through the clouds, he could see the brilliant blue of the ocean, dotted with the green of the Pacific Islands—the Solomons, Tarawa, Guadacanal.

With the heat shield facing the Earth, their view was mainly toward the rear, where a spectacular fireball of green, orange, and yellow, trailed out behind them like the tail of a comet.

Suddenly Collins noticed three huge orange and white blobs hovering outside his window. For a moment he was startled. What were these strange shapes? Not another UFO scare? Then he realized that the colored balls were their three reentry parachutes. They were floating now, coming safely down to Earth like a fall leaf landing on a pond.

"Apollo, this is Houston," Evans said. "Do you copy?"

"That's affirmative," Collins said.

The men in Building 30 got to their feet and cheered. Gene Kranz wiped the sweat from his brow. Deke Slayton leaned into the microphone, "Welcome back, boys," he said.

But the journey was not over yet. They still had to clear the final hurdle—a successful landing. Fifteen miles away, the carrier *Hornet* was waiting. Nearby, the recovery helicopter, with its crew of frogmen, was hovering.

Now all communications would shift from Houston to the *Hornet*.

"Apollo 11, Apollo 11, this is the *Hornet*, do you read?"

Armstrong spoke into his microphone: "Hello, *Hornet*. We read you loud and clear."

"Report on condition of the crew. Over."

Armstrong glanced at his men.

Gravity was dragging against their bodies, with full force. The weightlessness they had enjoyed in space was only a memory now. They hung heavily against their harness traps. They were tired, hot, and smelly. But they were almost home.

"Condition of the crew is excellent," Armstrong radioed back.

"We copy, Apollo. How does it look for splashdown?"

"Looks good, *Hornet*. We are coming in right on the splashdown point. We are at about 4,000 feet now, on the way down...3,000...2,500...that's 2,000...1,000..we're at 100 feet, coming up fast now..."

The CM hit the ocean like a ton of bricks and spun around, topsy-turvy, twirled by the surging waves and the ocean wind, which was blowing at a stiff 18 knots.

"We have splashdown!" Armstrong said triumphantly. It was 11:49, Houston time.

The helicopter pilot radioed in: "This is *Swim One*, Apollo 11, you're looking good. Our swimmers are in the water."

Three frogmen dropped from the chopper and swam around furiously under the whirling blades of the chopper, attaching the inflatable flotation collar around the CM.

Inside the module, the Apollo crew was getting a rough ride.

The CM was tossed around like a cork on the waves. Quickly, each of the astronauts downed a motion-sickness pill. This was no time for "stomach awareness."

After making sure the CM was safely afloat, the frogmen popped the hatch. One by one, the astronauts were hauled up into the hovering chopper. It was a little past one o'clock in the afternoon when, at last, they set foot on the carrier *Hornet*. From here the three men were whisked away to their quarters where they received what they had all longed for for so many days—a shower. The President had flown out to the carrier to welcome them back, and they shaved and tidied themselves up to meet him. Collins alone kept his "Moon mustache" as a souvenir of their incredible journey.

It was only when they were safely aboard the carrier, standing behind the protective glass of their quarantine enclosure, listening to President Nixon welcome them back, that Collins really appreciated that it was over.

They'd done it! They'd done what had seemed almost impossible —they'd successfully executed the ten critical maneuvers on his handwritten list. And more than that, they had sighted something strange on the surface of the Moon—something that moved and flew under its own power.

It was hard to decide which of the incredible events of the last few days was more unbelievable.

August 10, 1969

The astronauts returned to the Lunar Receiving Laboratory in Houston for two weeks of quarantine before they were permitted to rejoin their families. At last, the great day came. The NASA officials and the television cameras were there. But more important, the Collins, Aldrin, and Armstrong families had shown up in full force.

When Armstrong scooped his six-year-old son, Mark, up into his arms, the boy said, "Dad, how was it on the Moon?"

"It was strange and beautiful, Marky."

"Did you meet any Moon-men up there?"

"Sure," Armstrong said playfully.

The boy's eyes grew wide.

"You did? What did you do?"

Armstrong grinned.

"We invited them in for a cup of coffee and a piece of pie."

Mark laughed.

"Dad," he said, "you're silly."

Armstrong hoisted his son up onto his shoulders and walked toward home, his feet feeling the familiar grip of the Earth.

CHAPTER NINE

Harrison Grear, here. Now that you have read my story, you may be wondering which parts are fact and which are fiction.

You could say that the elements of my story range along a scale that is black at one end—the proven, documentable truth—and white on the other—purely in the realm of imaginative fiction.

The only part of the story that is absolute fiction are the dreams Collins and Aldrin had in Cislunar space. I made them up out of thin air. I also made up the recurring joke about inviting the aliens into the LM for coffee and pie. As far as I know, the lunch between Lovell, Slayton, and the astronauts did not happen as I have depicted it. These are shameless white lies.

On the black end of the scale, I have done my best to assure that all of the factual details of the flight are as accurate as I could make them. For these technical matters, I relied on a small mountain of books written by space experts and by the astronauts themselves. I was also fortunate to have written transcripts of the actual conversations between the astronauts and ground control.

I have included as much technical information as I thought possible because I believe that, in some ways, truth is stranger than fiction. The idea that the fate of the entire mission would hang on Armstrong's emergency switch repair with Buzz Aldrin's felt-tip pen made more dramatic sense than anything I could have thought up on my own.

As for the quotes in the story, I have taken some liberties here, rewriting what was said to fit the shape of the story. But I have relied very closely on the NASA transcriptions of the crew's conversations.

As for the actual sighting of the UFOs—this is where we start to get into the gray area in the middle. I can't tell you what the Apollo astronauts saw on their mission. I think that's up to *you* to decide.

I hope you have enjoyed my story. I'd like to think it has encouraged you to think more deeply about some of the great questions that face us as we enter the next century. I also hope that what I've written has helped, not hindered, our pursuit of the truth.

This is Harrison Grear, signing off...

Glossary

APOLLO 11
The first manned spacecraft to land on the Moon, on July 20, 1969.

ATMOSPHERE
Envelope of gaseous matter that surrounds a planet or star, held down by gravity. The Moon has no atmosphere so has no wind or weather either.

CIA
(CENTRAL INTELLIGENCE AGENCY)
U.S. agency set up in the late 1940s to protect the government from hostile foreign nations. The CIA employs agents in over 150 countries to send back information, which it then assesses, offering its analysis to other U.S. agencies. The CIA also attempts to prevent any risk to national security posed by foreign spies.

CISLUNAR SPACE
The area of space lying in between the orbits of the Earth and the Moon.

COLUMBIA
The code name for the Command Module used in the Apollo 11 mission.

CM
(COMMAND MODULE)
The only segment of Apollo 11 that returned to Earth after the Moon visit. The CM was equipped with a special heat-resistant shield to withstand the scorching temperatures it would face when traveling through our atmosphere. The cone-shaped module stood about 10 feet tall and 12 feet

wide at the base. Part of the craft was used to store the radio antennae and landing parachutes for use for the splashdown.

DESCENT ORBIT INSERTION
Stage of a lunar mission when astronauts have to leave the Command Module and travel down to the Moon's surface. This is executed by manning the Lunar Module and carefully descending to the intended landing place. While this is in process, the CM continues to orbit the Moon, waiting until the astronauts are ready to link up and then return to Earth.

EAGLE
The code name for the LM used to touch down on the surface of the Moon during the Apollo 11 mission.

EARTHSHINE
The Sun's light reflected back from the surface of the Earth.

EVA
(EXTRA-VEHICULAR ACTIVITY)
Astronaut movement, such as a Moon walk, that takes place outside the spacecraft.

GEMINI 7
Record-breaking space mission when crew members Jim Lovell and Frank Borman orbited the Earth for 14 days.

GEMINI 12
Space mission crewed by Buzz Aldrin and Jim Lovell, during which Aldrin made three space walks.

GRAVITY
Force that attracts bodies in the universe toward

each other. Gravity pulls everything on Earth toward the ground, making things feel heavy. On the Moon the force of gravity is weaker, making astronauts feel as if they weigh considerably lighter than they do on Earth.

HORNET
Aircraft carrier that rescued the parachuted Apollo 11 Command Module after it had splashed down in the Pacific Ocean.

LM
(LUNAR MODULE)
Joined to the Command Module by a tunnel, the LM (nicknamed "Eagle") was disconnected by the astronauts who used it to travel down to the lunar surface. When they had completed their investigations, Armstrong and Aldrin abandoned the LM in perpetual orbit around the Moon. Their lunar jeep was also left stranded on the planet's surface.

LUNAR ORBIT INSERTION
A period of deceleration, when the spacecraft attempts to fall into the orbit of the Moon. This is a very exact maneuver that could be potentially disastrous. The astronauts have to slow down enough for the craft to be harnessed into the Moon's gravity, but not so much that they come too close to it and risk crashing into the lunar surface.

MANNED SPACECRAFT CENTER
The base for the Apollo 11 mission to the Moon, situated in Houston. It was here that the astronauts prepared for the voyage and trained in special simulators. The ground control teams operated from the Center, and all contact between the spacecraft and Earth was channeled through this point.

MISSION CONTROL
The nucleus of the ground control for U.S. space missions. It is from here that NASA specialists and technicians guide the astronauts and spacecraft during flight.

MODULE
Part of a spacecraft that can be disconnected and split apart from the other segments.

NASA
(NATIONAL AERONAUTICS AND SPACE ADMINISTRATION)
U.S. government agency specializing in both aerial flight and space travel. Formed in 1958, NASA has accomplished many successful space flights, including the celebrated Apollo 11 mission in 1969. The agency also coordinates and researches projects involving unmanned satellites and space probes.

REENTRY
The instant that a spacecraft breaks back through the Earth's atmosphere on its return journey from space.

RENDEZVOUS
A mid-flight connection between two or more spacecraft.

SANTA CLAUS
Secret code word used by the NASA astronauts to warn Mission Control of any sightings of alien spacecraft.

SATURN V
Enormous rocket standing more than 360 feet tall, that was used to launch the Apollo 11 craft into space.

SM
(SERVICE MODULE)
Situated at the rear of the Command Module, the SM contained all the life-support systems for the Apollo 11 crew. It was discarded to orbit the Earth at the end of the voyage.

SPLASHDOWN
The moment when a spacecraft lands in the ocean.

TRANS-EARTH INJECTION
This stage of a lunar voyage is necessary in order to position the spacecraft back on course for Earth after visiting the Moon. The Lunar Module is abandoned, and the Command Module makes one powerful rocket burst to break out of the Moon's orbit and travel away from the planet.

TRANS-LUNAR INJECTION
The second rocket blast on a lunar mission, where the craft is pushed out of orbit around the Earth and set on course for the Moon.

UFO
(UNIDENTIFIED FLYING OBJECT)
Any unexplainable light or object that is seen in the sky or detected on radar.

BIOGRAPHIES

This story is a fictional account of a true-life mystery. Before you look at the facts and make up your own mind, here's a brief biography of the characters:

EDWARD E. ALDRIN, JR.—"BUZZ"
(ACTUAL CHARACTER)
Member of the three-man crew on the Apollo 11 mission. Also copilot of the Lunar Module.

NEIL ARMSTRONG
(ACTUAL CHARACTER)
Mission commander of Apollo 11 and the first man to walk on the Moon.

STEVE BALES
(ACTUAL CHARACTER)
Technical guidance officer at Mission Control for the Moon landing of the Apollo 11 Lunar Module.

CHARLES BERRY
(ACTUAL CHARACTER)
NASA medical director, in charge of ensuring the astronauts' fitness for the Apollo 11 flight.

MIKE COLLINS
(ACTUAL CHARACTER)
Crew member of the Apollo 11 team and pilot of the Command Module.

CHARLIE DUKE
(ACTUAL CHARACTER)
Spacecraft communicator during the landing phase of the Apollo mission, responsible for talking

of the Apollo mission, responsible for talking Armstrong and Aldrin through the descent of the Lunar Module down to the surface of the Moon.

RON EVANS
(ACTUAL CHARACTER)
Apollo 11 spacecraft communicator during the rendezvous between the Lunar Module and the Command Module, following the Moon landing.

HARRISON GREAR
(FICTIONAL)
Ageing reporter on the *Houston Sentinel*, who has been writing a column called 'Space Watch' for the last thirty years. As retirement looms before him, Grear decides to take a risk and finally tell the story of the Apollo 11 mission and expose the real truth about what took place.

FRED HAISE
(ACTUAL CHARACTER)
Back-up crew member of Apollo 11.

BEN HALEY
(FICTIONAL)
Late city editor of the *Houston Sentinel*, who taught Grear how to be an effective newshound.

GENE KRANZ
(ACTUAL CHARACTER)
Deke Slayton's partnering flight director of ground control for the Apollo 11 space mission.

JIM LOVELL
(ACTUAL CHARACTER)
Commander of the back-up crew for Apollo 11, but also a veteran astronaut himself. Lovell was a key crew member on the Gemini 7, 12 and Apollo 8 missions.

BRUCE McCANDLESS
(ACTUAL CHARACTER)

Spacecraft communicator back at Mission Control, maintaining radio contact with the Apollo astronauts.

DEKE SLAYTON
(ACTUAL CHARACTER)

Chief astronaut and head of all flight crews. Although unable to man a space mission actively himself due to medical problems, Slayton is universally admired by the astronauts for his guts and expertise.

CLASSIFIED FILES

Could it be possible that Apollo 11 was accompanied during its journey to the Moon? Are astronauts being observed from a distance by extraterrestrial beings? There are many conflicting reports, confirmations, and denials. Here are some of the arguments debating the truth of the alien encounter story:

An alien sighting really did take place during the Apollo 11 voyage because

According to former chief of NASA communications systems, Maurice Chatelain, Armstrong definitely reported seeing two UFOs on the rim of the Moon crater next to the Lunar Module. In 1979 he wrote:
The encounter was common knowledge in NASA, but nobody has talked about it until now.

According to author Timothy Good, in *Above Top Secret*, Dr. Vladimir Azhazha, a physicist and professor of mathematics at Moscow University, told Good that the encounter was reported immediately after the landing of the module but this message was never heard by the public — because NASA censored it. Good explains that although NASA technicians were able to screen radio transmissions which were released to the general public, amateur ham radio operators all over the world were able to listen in on the full conversation.

BUT:

Good asked Dr. Paul Lowman of NASA's Goddard Space Flight Center about the incident. Here is Lowman's reply:

Most of the radio communications from the Apollo crew on the surface were relayed in real time to Earth. I am continually amazed by people who claim that we have concealed the discovery of extraterrestrial activity on the Moon.
The confirmed discovery of extraterrestrial life, even if only by radio, will be the greatest scientific discovery of all time, and I speak without exaggeration. The idea that a civilian agency such as NASA, operating in the glare of publicity, could hide such a discovery is absurd, even if it wanted to. One would have to swear to secrecy not only the dozen astronauts who landed on the Moon but also the hundreds of engineers, technicians, and secretaries directly involved in the missions and communications links.

NASA admits that not *all* communications between the astronauts and ground control were made public. Why have some of the radio conversations been held back? Perhaps because the U.S. government knew that there was classified information on the part of the transcript that it couldn't afford to allow the public to hear. John MacLeaish, chief of public information at the Manned Spacecraft Center in Houston, told Good in 1970 that although there was no separate radio frequency used by NASA, private conversations with the astronauts, usually of a medical nature, could have been rerouted through different audio circuits on the ground so they would not be heard by the general public. But if the classified communications contain only routine discussions about the astronauts' health, why are they still being kept secret?

Former NASA scientist Otto Binder reportedly supported the claim that Neil Armstrong saw alien craft when the Eagle touched down on the lunar surface, with this account of the crucial conversation between Armstrong and Houston:

Mission Control: What's there? Mission Control calling Apollo 11.
Armstrong: These babies are huge, sir...
Enormous...Oh, God, you wouldn't believe it! I'm telling you, there are other spacecraft out there...lined up on the far side of the crater edge... They're on the Moon watching us...

Chatelain, Binder, and NASA scientist Dr. Garry Henderson, have all been quoted as stating that they have evidence suggesting that the government is hiding the truth from the American public. Chatelain wrote:

All Apollo and Gemini flights were followed, both at a distance and sometimes also quite closely, by space vehicles of extraterrestrial origin—flying saucers or UFOs...if you want to call them by that name. Every time it occurred, the astronauts informed Mission Control, who then ordered absolute silence.

I think Walter Schirra aboard Mercury 8 was the first of the astronauts to use the code name "Santa Claus" to indicate the presence of flying saucers next to space capsules. However, his announcements were barely noticed by the general public. It was a little different when James Lovell on board the Apollo 8 Command Module came out from behind the Moon and said for everyone to hear: "Please be informed that there is a Santa Claus." Even though this happened on Christmas Day 1968, many people sensed a hidden meaning in those words.

Timothy Good has also stated that Armstrong repeated his story after he had got back down to Earth. Good reports of a supposed conversation between Armstrong and an unnamed university professor at a NASA symposium after the flight (although Good acknowledges he did not personally witness the conversation, and that it might be apocryphal).

Professor: What really happened up there with Apollo 11?

Armstrong: It was incredible...of course, we had always known there was a possibility...the fact is, we were warned off...

Professor: What do you mean, "warned off"?

Armstrong: I can't go into details, except to say that their ships were far superior to ours in both size and technology—boy, were they big!...and menacing...

Professor: But NASA had other missions after Apollo 11?

Armstrong: Naturally—NASA was committed at that time and couldn't risk a panic on Earth...but it really was a quick scoop and back again.

BUT:

Later, Good wrote Armstrong a letter, asking for him to confirm the story. When the astronaut replied, Good was disappointed to read that he categorically denied the reported conversation had ever taken place. Armstrong also pointed out very clearly that he had neither been involved in any kind of coverup, nor witnessed any alien craft.

An alien sighting didn't take place during the Apollo 11 voyage because

The majority of the evidence supporting the alien story is made up of secondhand witness reports—merely people's opinions. Without the full transcript of the dialogue between ground control and the Apollo crew during the mission, there can be no substantial proof that the alien sighting is authentic. Although Tim Good has argued that Neil Armstrong himself told someone at NASA that he had seen alien craft, this is just hearsay. Any firsthand evidence that we do have from Armstrong totally contradicts Good's claims. Armstrong wrote to Good:

Your "reliable sources" are unreliable. There were no objects reported, found, or seen on Apollo 11 or any other Apollo flight other than of natural origin. All observations on all Apollo flights were fully reported to the public.

BUT:

Possibly there is a reason why Neil Armstrong has not publicly spoken about the UFO story. If such a fantastic encounter really did take place, the U.S. government would want to keep it secret. Although he may have unofficially spoken the truth to NASA insiders, perhaps Armstrong was warned to keep his experience to himself. After all, the government simply could not afford to cope with the panic and uproar that would follow if people found out about the alien sighting.

Too many people were involved in the Apollo 11 project for such an amazing story to have been kept quiet for so long. As Dr. Lowman said, a mission to the Moon requires a vast support team on the ground. The huge backup crew would been made up of countless office workers, scientists, and technical teams. If the alien story is really true—why haven't more witnesses come forward?

Even if it could be proved that the astronauts really did report seeing extraterrestrial craft, this does not mean that aliens exist. It would only prove that the astronauts *thought* that they saw them.

When the Apollo and Gemini missions first took place, no one was really sure what space travel felt like and what effects it could have on astronauts. In the unique environment on board the spacecraft, it is possible that the crew could have been more susceptible to the idea that they were not alone. Perhaps after many long and tiring hours in Cislunar space the men hallucinated that they were being accompanied by UFOs. Maybe they saw something unfamiliar in the distance and let their imaginations do the rest. Whatever the astronauts *thought* they witnessed, there is no scientific evidence to prove that they really *were* in the company of an extraterrestrial presence.

THE BATTLE TO REACH THE STARS

What is it in the human condition that longs for alien contact? Simple cosmic loneliness? An insatiable thirst for knowledge, or just boredom with everyday life?

It would appear that we moderns are not the only ones who have felt this compulsion. The sighting of extraterrestrials, and accounts of their landings, have been recorded since ancient Biblical times. Legends of their visits survive in the folklore of a thousand different cultures. And yet, why is it that we have not seen a single solid shred of evidence that would confirm that we have made contact with "someone upstairs," as Deke Slayton would say?

Perhaps we need to continue our exploration of the universe much farther before we can finally find the answer to the UFO question. Only then will we discover once and for all if alien sightings are the product of fantasy or reality.

Could it be that after watching our infantile ancestors crawl over the Earth for millions of years, our alien neighbors feel we have evolved sufficiently to be of interest to them at long last? Now that human beings are beginning to take their first tentative steps into space travel, possibly we are being observed and monitored during these early missions?

If this is the case, in order to prophesy what the future holds for us, perhaps we need to examine how we've got this far.

EARLY SATELLITES

The modern space era began on October 4, 1957, when the then Soviet Union stunned the world by launching *Sputnik*, a small globe of metal about two feet in diameter, weighing about 180 pounds. It circled the Earth for one hour and thirty six minutes, sending back the first satellite messages from space.

Two weeks later, the Soviets capped their success by launching *Sputnik II*, a much larger satellite, weighing about 1,100 pounds and carrying a passenger—a dog named "Laika." As the satellite circled the Earth, data about the dog's condition was relayed back to Earth. Laika died after about 100 hours in orbit.

THE SPACE RACE

Although U.S. scientists had been working on the concept of space flight, they were not prepared for the triumphant success of their Soviet competitors. It was true, the United States had recruited Werner von Braun and other German scientists to adapt the German *V-2* rocket for peacetime use. In 1949, the United States had successfully launched a rocket that had traveled to a record height of 240 miles above the Earth's surface. But the sudden news of the Soviet success began what is now known as the Space Race, a competition between two immense superpowers for the technological dominance of outer space.

Stung by the exploits of the Soviets, President Dwight Eisenhower laid the groundwork for creating NASA and ordered that the U.S. Space Program should be kicked into high gear.

Two months after the launch of *Sputnik I*, NASA had cobbled together a satellite, *Explorer I*, which was about the size of a grapefruit and weighed only three pounds. When the day of the launch arrived, television and newspaper cameras from all over the world were trained on the *Vanguard* rocket as it sat on its launchpad at Cape Canaveral, Florida (later to be named Cape Kennedy). At the moment of ignition, the huge rocket rose only four feet from the pad before it toppled and exploded in a spectacular fireball.

From this humiliating beginning, the United States entered an ambitious program of space flight that would eventually carry men to the Moon. Over the next decade, with the help of scientists and technicians from Britain, France, Canada, and Italy, NASA would hurl more than 400 satellites into space.

But it was *manned* spaceflight that had captured the public's imagination.

THE FIRST ASTRONAUTS

In a desperate battle between the two superpowers, the U.S. and Soviet space programs were set at full speed in a determined bid to send the first man to the Moon.

With an ear to the ground, on April 9, 1959, NASA announced the selection of the first U.S. astronauts, who came to be known as the "Original Seven." They were all military men and highly skilled pilots. Among them was an air force captain named Donald Slayton. His friends called him "Deke." The others would also become important players in the drama of the Space Race.

On April 12, 1961, the Soviets again scored a first by putting the first man into orbit. Cosmonaut Yuri Gagarin rode his *Vostok* spacecraft at a record speed of 17,398 miles per hour and circled the Earth for over an hour. He radioed back:

The sky looks very, very dark and the Earth is bluish.

He became the first human to see the planet from the reaches of space.

Racing hard to catch up, the US launched its first manned flight on May 5, 1961. Astronaut Alan Shepard made a 15 minute low-atmosphere orbital flight and splashed down safely in the Atlantic. Even though it appeared that the US was lagging behind, Shepard's mission had proved one thing – the United States was still in the game.

On May 25, 1961, during his Second State of the Union Address, President John F. Kennedy prompted the US Space Program to make a quantum leap when he stated:

I believe that this nation should commit itself to achieving the goal, before this decade is out, of landing a man on the Moon and returning him safely to Earth.

Publicly, the announcement was met with a groundswell of approval. Americans were tired of seeing their astronauts coming up second best, as one newspaper reporter told Kennedy at a news conference. "No one is more tired than I am," Kennedy shot back. And he took action to reverse the trend.

Privately, the President's challenge was met with a mixture of pride and dismay by the officials at NASA. They could not see how it was feasible for the US government to attempt to send astronauts to the Moon before the end of the decade. After all, NASA was still exploding rockets on the launch pad!

Analysts now agree that the race to the Moon was not a sound decision from a scientific viewpoint. It was basically a public relations gambit, a "flagpoles and footprints" mission aimed at proving technological superiority. It would have made far more sense for the United States and Soviet Union to join forces in building a space station. But the politics of the Cold War era, and the bull-headed determination of the superpower leaders, made such cooperation unthinkable back in 1961.

THE U.S. STRUGGLE FOR THE MOON

The U.S. Space Program was mapped out in three stages:
1. **Project Mercury** was aimed at mastering the technology of orbital flight.
2. **Gemini** was focused on space walks and docking maneuvers.
3. **Apollo** was concerned with the specifics of landing a man on the Moon.

The Moon Race totally overshadowed other space achievements. The United States' assumption that the Soviets were aiming for the Moon had no firm foundation. After a flurry of successes, the Soviet Union dropped out of the race in 1965. They simply ran out of technological know-how and decided to turn their attention to other aspects of space travel.

Meanwhile, NASA was moving ahead with astonishing speed and clarity. With every mission, NASA was getting closer to the ultimate goal of sending an American to the Moon.

On February 20, 1962, John Glenn became the first astronaut in space. Flying much higher than Alan Shepard, he orbited the Earth for more than four hours.

Edward White made the first space walk in 1965. Frank Borman and James Lovell also orbited the Earth for a record-breaking 14 days in December of that year. Neil Armstrong made the first space docking in 1966, and Buzz Aldrin made a successful two and a half hour space walk.

BUT:

1967 was a year of tragedy for both the U.S. and Soviet space explorers. Three Apollo 1 astronauts were killed in a fire during a routine, on-the-ground training exercise at Cape Kennedy. A spark from damaged wiring ignited the oxygen-rich atmosphere in their capsule. A faulty latch on the door prevented them from escaping the firestorm that snuffed out their lives. Meanwhile, a Soviet spacecraft orbiting the Earth crashed when the parachute failed to open during reentry, killing Cosmonaut Vladimir Komarov.

By 1968, the U.S. Space Program was back on track. On Christmas Day, Frank Borman, James Lovell, and William Anders captured the public imagination with a spectacular flight that included ten lunar orbits.

Finally NASA's dream was realized when Neil Armstrong set foot on the lunar surface on July 20, 1969. Armstrong and his crewmates Mike Collins and Buzz Aldrin had won the Moon race—in front of an audience of half a billion TV viewers.

BUT:

By the time the Apollo 11 crew actually landed on the Moon, the American public had accepted space flight as an almost routine undertaking. Some had begun to question whether the money might be better spent on resolving some of the major streets, economic woes and a disastrous war in Vietnam.

The inevitable budget cuts began to slow down the Space Program. The Apollo flights ran out of funding in 1972 after NASA had made six lunar landings. Politicians had turned their attention to other matters. Public apathy had set in. The most absurd example of this came during the later Apollo flights, when the national television networks refused to disrupt their afternoon programming of commercials and soap operas to carry live coverage of the astronauts in space.

THE MOON AND BEYOND

Following the success of Apollo 11, scientists began looking at other means of deepening their knowledge of space exploration. Although interest in the American Space Program waned, the Soviets were patiently plugging away, launching a continuous stream of successful flights and deepening their knowledge of space travel.

In 1975, Deke Slayton, who had been grounded during the entire Space Race by a heart murmur, finally made his first flight during a joint Soviet-American mission which involved docking two craft while they orbited the Earth – working together in a way that would have been unthinkable during the Cold War years.

The Soviets began work on their space station, 'Mir'. The US began its 'Skylab' programme, creating an orbiting space station which could be used for extended experiments in space with astronauts working and living on board. The 1970s also saw the introduction of the concept of the Space Shuttle – the first re-usable spacecraft. Then, on January 28, 1986, NASA suffered its worst catastrophe. Despite repeated warnings from rocket experts, the Shuttle 'Challenger', was from rocket experts, the Shuttle "Challenger" was launched on a bitterly cold morning at the Cape. The shuttle rose from the pad, soared briefly and then suddenly exploded, killing seven astronauts, including a civilian grade school teacher. It was a death knell for the manned flight program.

Although the Soviets had not landed on the Moon, they had launched eight space stations since the mid-1970s. In 1988, cosmonaut Yuri Romanenko set a space endurance record—326 days on board "Mir"—nearly four times the U.S. record. The Russians continued to plow funds into space research after the breakup of the Soviet Union, setting their sights on Mars. Although the United States sent a series of *Viking* probes to the red planet, the Russian scientists plan to land an unmanned vehicle there by the year 2000.

Russia is not the only player in the drama. Led by the French and the Germans, the European Space Agency has developed sophisticated space vehicles. The Japanese and Chinese have also developed their own space programs.

But what about the future?

SPACE EXPLORATION IN THE FUTURE

AMERICA'S AMBITIONS IN SPACE

Following the "Challenger" tragedy, Dr. Sally Ride, the first American woman in space, wrote a report entitled *Leadership and America's Future in Space*:

For nearly a quarter of a century, the U.S. Space Program enjoyed what can appropriately be termed a "golden age." The United States was clearly and unquestionably the leader in space exploration.

However, in the aftermath of the "Challenger" accident, reviews of our Space Program made its shortcomings starkly apparent. The U.S. civilian Space Program is now at a crossroads.

Dr. Ride thought it was pointless to use space exploration as a military tool. Space travel offers so many learning opportunities, Ride argued, it would be a waste to return to the Cold War days when the Soviet and U.S. governments secretly competed in space technology.

Instead, Ride has suggested that the Space Program could provide the answers to some of the planet's most pressing global problems. So in 1986, President Ronald Reagan commissioned Ride and others to come up with a blueprint for the future of the Space Program.

A key part of the policy they came up with was "Project Pathfinder"—a guide for future space missions. The project had four key goals:

1. **Mission to Planet Earth** plans for an orbital observation system to be launched that would

give scientists a better understanding of how the Earth functions as a planet.

2. **Exploration of the Solar System** features an unmanned exploration of Mars. A robotic mission to the planet would bring back samples of Martian soil by the year 2000.

3. **Human to Mars** calls for a manned landing on the Martian surface by the year 2010.

4. **Outpost on the Moon** would entail the establishment of a permanent base on the lunar surface, where as many as 30 people could live and work for extended periods of time. Buzz Aldrin suggested that erecting solar panels on the Moon might be a high-tech answer to the energy crisis on Earth.

A CHANCE TO MEET OUR NEIGHBORS?

The further we develop our knowledge of the solar system and beyond, the higher the odds that we may come across information that could resolve the UFO question. Surely as we delve deeper and deeper into the dark realms of space, we must stand a greater chance of encountering other nonhuman forms of life? Scientists are constantly sending satellites and radio waves enormous distances away from Earth. How long before our transmissions stumble upon a life-supporting craft or planet? Or that we receive a return signal? Many scientists argue that the odds of finding extraterrestrial life are greater than the odds against. Our own solar system contains 9 planets, 39 moons, and the Sun. The Sun is only one of over 100 billion stars in the Milky Way Galaxy, each with its own collection of planets and moons, much like ours. But it doesn't stop there. The Milky Way is only one of perhaps ten billion known galaxies.

It is difficult to believe that out of all these

worlds, spread across the vast reaches of the cosmos, our tiny blue planet is the only one that has evolved an intelligent, adventurous, endlessly curious creature such as ourselves.

But maybe some of us already have the knowledge that there are other life forms in addition to ourselves?

There are many well-documented sightings of UFOs by pilots and astronauts.

A British magazine named *Encounters* ran a story called "Confessions of an Astronaut" in their October 1995 issue. They quoted several pilots who confirmed their belief that the objects they had seen were truly unexplained flying objects.

Perhaps the most dramatic testimony comes from Major Gordon Cooper, one of the original Mercury Seven astronauts and the last man to fly in space alone.
A letter said to be from Cooper was read at a meeting of the United Nations, urging examination of the growing fund of evidence about the attempts of extraterrestrials to make contact with members of the human species:
I believe that these extraterrestrial vehicles and their crews are visiting this planet from other planets.
J.L. Ferrando reported in 1973 that Cooper said, in an interview that:
For many years I have lived with a secret, in a secrecy imposed on all specialists in astronautics. I can now reveal that every day, in the United States, our radar instruments capture objects of form and composition unknown to us. And there are thousands of witness reports and a quantity of documents to prove this, but nobody wants to

make them public.
So even though many intelligent, trained pilots and astronauts have positively testified that UFOs *do* exist, these people have not felt able to speak about their discoveries.

Could the government be deliberately hiding this knowledge? Even though many feel that Buzz Aldrin clearly documented the Apollo 11 UFO sighting, he is more cautious about acknowledging it as an authentic alien encounter. In his report, he never claims that he saw anything but a strange, unidentified shape, which could possibly even have been a part of their own spacecraft. And, as he says in his book: **We let the matter drop right there.**

It seems that the Apollo astronauts did not feel able to explain to the world exactly what they saw. Maybe they had been warned that extraordinary sightings were classified—to be kept secret at all costs.

Why? Major Gordon Cooper is said to have told J.L. Ferrando that secrecy is maintained:
Because the authorities are afraid that people may think of God-knows-what kind of horrible invaders. So the password still is: "We have to avoid the panic by any means."

THE UFO PHENOMENON

Despite thousands of claims of UFO sightings, hundreds of stories of UFO abductions, and dozens of tales of crashed alien spaceships, there is not a single solid piece of evidence that, conclusively proves the existence of life on other planets. Nonetheless, the stories survive. It may be that the search for extraterrestrial life is an essential element of the human psyche, an instinctive need that must be satisfied.

THE OFFICIAL VERDICT

As a way of responding to the UFO fervor, the air force commissioned a study entitled *Project Blue Book,* which made an exhaustive review of the UFO sightings. In 1969 the air force issued a summation:

**THERE IS NO EVIDENCE THAT THE SIGHTED OBJECTS ARE OF AN EXTRATERRESTRIAL NATURE.
CASE CLOSED.**

It seems a very brash way of discrediting any possibility of alien life, but perhaps the report makes a fair summation of the evidence. If beings from another planet really wanted to contact us, their greeting would be no secret. They would certainly have the means to make their wishes known without endangering themselves.

EPILOGUE

It seems that the Apollo 11 is just one of a myriad of UFO encounters that the government wants us to forget. It seems impossible to find any concrete answers to the mystery. Even the astronauts themselves have offered conflicting evidence about what they saw.

A final twist to the debate comes directly out of my own experience. In November 1995, when I was preparing the manuscript for this book, I chanced to see a small ad in our local paper announcing that Jim Lovell was scheduled to appear at a Houston bookstore to promote his book, *Lost Moon*, a thrilling account of the perilous journey of Apollo 13.

With the *Encounters* magazine tucked under my arm, I went down to the bookstore to meet Lovell for the first time. Although I had written many stories about his flights, I had never actually met the man during my years of reporting. Now was my chance.

When I entered the store I saw a distinguished, well-dressed man seated at a polished wooden table, signing books and chatting with a crowd of admirers. It was Lovell.

I waited a respectful amount of time until the crowd had dissipated, then came forward and introduced myself, explaining that this book project was something I had meant to do for several years and was just now completing.

"What's your book about?" Lovell asked.

When I told him, he laughed good-naturedly.

"There are no UFOs," he said simply.

I slipped the magazine from under my arms and laid it out on the table, pointing out the places in

the article that quoted him as a discoverer of
UFOs.

Lovell adjusted his glasses and read silently for
a few moments. It was very quiet in the bookstore.
I couldn't tell if I had offended him or not. But I
knew I wasn't there to win a popularity contest, I
was there to ferret out the truth.

Lovell put down his glasses and looked at me.
Again, I heard his pleasant chuckle.

"This is all fiction," he said.

He sat back in his chair and arched his eyebrows.
"Look, I am not saying that there isn't intelligent
life somewhere else in the universe. All I'm saying
is that they haven't contacted us yet. If these
beings have the technology to do all of the things
people say they can do, they would certainly have
the ability to contact us and make their presence
known. They just have not done that."

With that cryptic remark, he took a copy of *Lost
Moon* from the table and bent over it with his
ballpoint pen. He closed the book and handed it to
me with a wink.

"Just between you and me, I put a little
message in there for you," he said.

I thanked him, paid for the book at the cash
desk and walked out of the store, my head
swimming with the twists and turns of the story I
was attempting to write.

I was so deeply engrossed in thought that I didn't
think to look at Lovell's inscription until I was in
the car driving home. Stopped at a red light, I
suddenly remembered and flipped the book open.
In the reddish glare of the traffic light, I read
what he had written in a relaxed, flowing hand:

There are no UFOs!
Jim Lovell

Lovell has his reasons for denying any extraterrestrial contact, but I can't agree.

I don't know if I will live long enough to see the day when humans will extend their hands and grip the exotic limbs of an alien being in a sign of friendship. I don't know if I will be around to witness the first intraterrestrial conversation. I do think that some day it will come.

When it arrives, I hope our fellow travelers in the cosmos find us to be friendly neighbors and good companions in our journey among the stars. Only then will the government be forced to throw open its files and admit the truth.

BIBLIOGRAPHY

Aldrin, Buzz, *Men From Earth*. New York: Doubleday, 1989.

Return To Earth. New York: Random House, 1973.

Armstrong, Neil, *First On The Moon*. Boston: Little, Brown and Co., 1970.

Bryan, C.D.B. *Close Encounters of the Fourth Kind*. New York, Alfred Knopf, 1995.

Collins, Michael, *Carrying The Fire*. New York: Farrar, Straus and Giroux, 1974.

Chatelain, Maurice, *Our Ancestors Came From Outer Space*. New York: Dell Publishing Co., 1975.

Cousineau, Phil, *UFO*. New York: HarperCollins, 1995.

Furniss, Tim, *Manned Spaceflight Log*. London: Jane's Publishing Co., 1983.

Good, Timothy, *Above Top Secret*. London: HarperCollins, 1989.

Hurt, Harry, *For All Mankind*, New York: Atlantic Monthly Press, 1988.

Lovell, Jim, *Lost Moon*. New York: Houghton Mifflin, 1994.

Murray, Charles, *Apollo: The Race to the Moon*. New York: Simon & Schuster, 1989.

Randles, Jenny, *UFO Retrievals*. London; Blanford, 1995.

Sitchin, Zecharia, *Genesis Revisted*. New York: Avon Books, 1990.

Spencer, John, *The UFO Encyclopedia*. London: Headline, 1990.

Encounters, Issue 1, October 1995. Dorset: Paragon Publishing, 1995.

CLASSIFIED

Reader, your brief is to be on the alert for the following spine-tingling books.

CLASSIFIED SERIES:

☐ The Internet Incident	Ian Probert	£3.99
☐ Encounter on the Moon	Robin Moore	£3.99
☐ Discovery at Roswell	Terry Deary	£3.99
☐ The Philadelphia Experiment	Terry Deary	£3.99
☐ The Nuclear Winter Man	Terry Deary	£3.99
☐ Break Out!	Terry Deary	£3.99
☐ Area 51	Robin Moore	£3.99
☐ Virus Outbreak	Ian Probert	£3.99

Stay tuned for further titles. Over and out.